FINANCIAL FORTRESS

FINANCIAL FORTRESS

A Retirement Plan Engineered to Withstand
Market Risk, Taxes, Inflation, and Life

Ira S. Koyner

Published by Triathlon Partners Media LLC

Triathlon
Partners
Media LLC

www.TriathlonPartners.com

ISBN: 979-8-218-93278-7

Printed in the United States of America

REGULATORY DISCLAIMER

This book is for informational and educational purposes only and does not constitute investment, legal, or tax advice. The views expressed are those of the author and do not necessarily reflect the opinions or positions of Triathlon Partners LLC, a registered investment adviser with the State of Connecticut. Registration as an investment adviser does not imply any level of skill or training.

The mention of Triathlon Partners LLC in this book is for informational purposes only and should not be construed as an endorsement, recommendation, or solicitation of its services or of any specific investment, security, insurance contract, or strategy.

Investing involves risk, including the potential loss of principal. Past performance is not indicative of future results. Structured products, annuities, insurance contracts, real estate exchanges, and other strategies discussed may involve market risk, credit risk, liquidity constraints, tax implications, and complexity that may not be appropriate for all investors.

Insurance guarantees are subject to the claims-paying ability of the issuing insurer. Tax laws and regulations are subject to change and may vary by jurisdiction.

Any examples of investment strategies, case studies, or financial outcomes discussed in this book are for illustrative purposes only and may not reflect actual results or be suitable for any particular individual. Readers should consult with qualified financial, tax, and legal professionals before implementing any strategy discussed herein.

Neither the author, the publisher, nor Triathlon Partners LLC makes any representations or warranties as to the accuracy or completeness of the information contained herein and assumes no liability for any loss arising from its use. The author may have a financial interest in the investments or strategies discussed. References to specific securities, asset classes, or strategies should not be interpreted as recommendations or endorsements.

Acknowledgments

This book exists because I was given the space, support, and encouragement to pursue work that demands patience, focus, and conviction.

First and always, I am grateful to my wife. Her love, steadiness, and belief made it possible for me to dedicate time and energy to something I care deeply about. Nothing in this book would exist without the foundation she provides every day. I am equally thankful to my children, whose curiosity, perspective, and presence are a constant reminder of why thoughtful planning matters beyond numbers and charts.

I owe a great deal to my parents, teachers, and mentors I have been fortunate to learn from over the years. They taught me not simply what to think, but how to think, how to question assumptions, challenge conventions, and remain intellectually curious even when consensus feels comfortable. Their influence is visible throughout.

I am also grateful to those who doubted me. Skepticism has a way of sharpening ideas and strengthening resolve. Being questioned forced me to refine my thinking, work harder, and articulate why structure, discipline, and judgment matter more than slogans or shortcuts.

Professionally, this book reflects years of conversation, planning work, and observation. I am thankful to the clients who trusted me with complex decisions and allowed me to learn alongside them. I also owe a debt to the attorneys, accountants, insurance professionals, and investment advisors who tested assumptions, debated trade-offs, and reinforced the importance of integrated thinking.

While any errors or omissions are mine alone, the ideas in this book were shaped by people who understand that good financial planning is rarely about products, and almost always about judgment.

Table of Contents

Preface: Planning for the World We Actually Live In

For most of my professional life, I managed foreign exchange options portfolios at large global banks. This was not academic or theoretical risk. It was a real risk, measured in probabilities, potential losses, and outcomes under stress.

Portfolios had to perform in conditions most people never consider: volatility spikes, evaporating liquidity, cross-asset contagion, and central bank intervention.

In that world, no one cared how portfolios performed when markets behaved as expected. The focus was always on what happened when they didn't. Hope and prayer were not acceptable risk-management strategies. Stress testing was routine, and risk was engineered in advance to limit losses, not if, but when, assumptions failed.

The risk management tools were complex, but the mindset was simple: define exposure, understand failure points, and never assume the market will cooperate.

Ironically, I never applied that same mindset to my own financial life. I had never turned the lens on myself. Time made that easy to avoid. My workdays routinely exceeded eleven hours. I spent nearly four hours commuting between Connecticut and Manhattan. I was not disengaged from my finances. I did what many people do and delegated to credentialed advisors.

Investments were managed.
Insurance was in place.
Retirement accounts were funded.
I was committed to saving.
On paper, every box was checked.

The inflection point came in 2020. COVID eliminated my commute and created something rare: time to think.

For the first time, I examined my finances not through the lens of account balances, net worth, or annual returns, but as a single, integrated system. I stress-tested allocations, tax strategies, pre-tax vs post-tax retirement contributions, insurance structures, retirement timing, mortality assumptions, and cash-flow variability. I analyzed my personal finances with the same scrutiny I had applied for decades managing institutional risk.

The exercise was sobering.
When real stress arrives, how does my plan hold up?

> Volatility: If markets fall 30 percent as I approach or are in early retirement, is there a structural backstop, or does the plan assume unwavering discipline?
>
> Taxes: What will my account balances actually translate into in after-tax, dependable income? Have Roth conversions, RMD projections, and withdrawal sequencing been modeled together, or are they being handled separately? A single uncoordinated withdrawal can cascade across brackets, Medicare premiums, and Social Security taxation simultaneously.
>
> Inflation: If the cost of living rises 40 percent over five years, does my income keep pace, or does the plan fall behind while the statement balance still looks fine?
>
> Non-market risk: If I pass away or become incapacitated, does the plan keep functioning? Is there infrastructure in place to replace lost income, fund care costs, and provide liquidity without forcing asset sales at the worst possible time?

Is there a plan here, or just a collection of products?

What I found was structural, not incidental.

My advisors had not built a coordinated plan. They had managed components. There was a disconnect between how assets were accumulated and what they were expected to accomplish. Each operated competently within their own sphere, but no one was engineering the structure. The fragmentation remained invisible until everything was viewed as a whole.

The structural failures were evident not only in what I owned, but in what was conspicuously absent.

My investment portfolio was more volatile than necessary for a moderate-to-conservative profile. In good years, it merely met expectations. In bad years, there was no structural backstop. "Diversification" meant adding bonds that created tax drag or reaching for yield in illiquid or complex strategies that were difficult to unwind when flexibility and liquidity were needed.

When market stress created an opportunity, I didn't feel positioned to respond. Account balances were falling, the portfolio felt fragile, and acting seemed riskier than waiting. The ability to adjust had disappeared. What was built and what was needed were no longer aligned.

Insurance revealed similar fragmentation. My family accumulated many policies, each purchased to address a specific need. None were optimized toward a unified objective. Large whole life policies were overfunded but not structured for tax-efficient income. Term insurance was concentrated, not laddered. Survivorship insurance was never introduced. For my son's special needs trust, it was the coverage that mattered most, and no one ever brought it up. Long-term care was handled separately at significant cost.

When questions arose about premiums, structure, or fine print, the proposed solution was to add another policy, not to redesign existing ones.

Retirement planning followed a similar pattern. "401(k) all the way" was the default. Converting account balances into after-tax income was not discussed. Future tax consequences were shelved. Charitable giving wasn't addressed.

The problem was not effort. It was structure.
Advice was siloed.
Decisions were disconnected.
Optimization was assumed rather than engineered.

Silos do more than magnify misalignment. They restrict opportunity, erode flexibility, and compound inefficiency.

Once I redesigned my plan, shifting from component management to coordinated design, the impact was immediate. Volatility was reduced. Tax reduction strategies were implemented. Inflation was addressed. Insurance was optimized. My retirement plan finally functioned as one system.

As I shared this realization and the changes I made with family and friends, a pattern emerged. My situation was not unique. Their "plans" were also collages of well-intentioned products that worked only if markets and life cooperated.

They asked if I could assist with their planning. That is when I started my firm. I left the trading desk for something that felt considerably more meaningful. The largest trade I ever made was walking away from foreign exchange. No regrets.

This book exists because behavior is imperfect, fragmentation snowballs, and disconnection breeds inefficiencies. Coordination transforms isolated decisions into a cohesive system.

A fortress is engineered to endure stress. Retirement should be engineered the same way.

Introduction: A Retirement Plan Is a System

Most retirement plans look finished. The balances are diversified. The advisor said everything is fine. The quarterly statements confirm it.

What the statements do not show is the embedded tax liability inside the IRA, the Social Security decision that permanently reduces survivor income, or the conversion window that narrows each year while the balance keeps growing. None of these is reckless. Each one made sense on its own. They were simply never analyzed together.

A coordinated plan using the same assets and the same time horizon, viewed as one system rather than a set of separate decisions, can increase retirement spending by more than 25 percent without reducing what is left to heirs after tax. That result does not require exotic strategies. It comes from architecture.

Retirement rarely breaks for one reason. It breaks when several risks arrive together and the plan was built as if they would come one at a time. I spent nearly three decades designing and trading currency options, where the working assumption was that markets do not cooperate under stress. A retirement plan has to survive under the same conditions. You do not build a fortress and hope for good weather. You build it to withstand the storm.

This book is structured as five acts around the four risks that can break a plan: volatility, taxes, inflation, and the non-market events that get the least attention and cause the most damage. Each act builds on the one before it. The capstones at the end of each act show the concepts working together. If you want a structure that holds through bad markets, tax surprises, rising costs, and the transition to a surviving spouse, keep reading. If you want stock picks or a five-step checklist, read something else.

The gap between what a plan appears to be and what it can actually deliver is what this book is about.

Reading This Book Your Way

Throughout the book, several recurring callouts signal specific types of content:

Early Decision Rule: the principle that frames the chapter. Read these even if you skim.

Reality Check: a direct challenge to a common assumption. Intentionally blunt.

Rule Extracted: the lesson distilled from a case study or example.

What This Means for You: the practical takeaway translated from a case study into your own planning.

Design Choice Checkpoint: a decision point where the right answer depends on the specific plan, not a universal rule.

Ask Your Advisor Today: questions designed to be brought verbatim into a planning meeting. If your advisor cannot answer them clearly, that is useful information.

Integration Check: the questions that close each act, connecting decisions across chapters into a single coordinated review.

ACT I: Volatility and Portfolio Design

Most financial planning begins with reasonable assumptions: markets rise over time, diversification smooths returns, discipline holds under pressure, and time will always allow for recovery. Those ideas are sensible, but they do not tell the whole story. This act begins where many plans become fragile: in the gap between how markets behave and how investors respond. It then builds the portfolio design that addresses that gap.

Chapter 1: Volatility, Behavior, and Why Diversification Falls Short

> **Early Decision Rule:**
> Market declines usually do not destroy plans by themselves. The damage comes from the decisions volatility pressures investors to make.

When markets sell off and account balances fall, investors are pushed into uncomfortable decisions. They may sell, freeze, move to safety, or abandon a strategy in the middle of the cycle. Even experienced and disciplined investors struggle to remain objective when uncertainty dominates headlines. That is how a temporary market decline becomes lasting planning damage.

Plan for Volatility Before It Arrives

Volatility management is less about prediction than preparation. At some level of stress, people abandon plans that felt sensible when markets were calm. Risk cannot be eliminated, but volatility can be reduced to a level that makes investor behavior more predictable. A retirement plan that anticipates volatility keeps investors invested.

Volatility Is Normal

Market volatility is not rare; it is a permanent feature of investing. Since 1997, the S&P 500 has gone through repeated drawdowns, some brief and some severe. Long-term charts smooth these episodes into upward-sloping lines. However, investors experience volatility in the moment. Falling balances, ugly headlines, and uncertainty about what comes next test discipline. That is when long-term plans can derail.

S&P 500 Significant Declines, 1997–2026

Peak	Event	Trough	Decline
Oct 1997	Asian Financial Crisis	Oct 1997	**−11%**
Jul 1998	Russian Debt Default / LTCM Collapse	Aug 1998	**−19%**
Mar 2000	Dot-Com Bust	Oct 2002	**−49%**
Oct 2007	Global Financial Crisis	Mar 2009	**−57%**
Apr 2010	Flash Crash / Eurozone Debt Stress	Jul 2010	**−16%**
Apr 2011	U.S. Credit Downgrade / Eurozone Crisis	Oct 2011	**−19%**
May 2015	China Devaluation / Oil Collapse	Feb 2016	**−14%**
Jan 2018	Volatility Shock	Apr 2018	**−10%**
Sep 2018	Fed Tightening / Trade War Escalation	Dec 2018	**−20%**
Feb 2020	COVID-19 Global Shutdown	Mar 2020	**−34%**
Jan 2022	Inflation Shock / Rapid Rate Tightening	Oct 2022	**−25%**
Feb 2023	Regional Banking Stress	Mar 2023	**−8%**
Feb 2025	Tariff Escalation Shock	Apr 2025	**−19%**

Footnote: Source: SPY ETF closing prices (price return only; dividends excluded). Dates and percentage changes are illustrative and reflect index-level moves, not client performance. Indexes are unmanaged and cannot be invested in directly. This is not a guarantee of results. See Regulatory Disclaimer / Appendix Disclosures.

Volatility and Sequence-of-Returns Risk

Volatility becomes more dangerous as retirement approaches and especially once withdrawals begin. At that stage, sequence risk, the order in which gains and losses occur, can matter more than average returns. Two portfolios can earn the same average return and still produce very different outcomes depending on when losses occur. In retirement, those losses are more damaging because withdrawals continue while the portfolio is down, permanently removing capital from the recovery.

The mathematics of recovery is unforgiving. A forty percent decline on a $100 account takes the balance to $60. A forty percent gain from $60 only rises to $84, not back to $100. On paper, the average return looks like zero, but the investor is still sixteen percent below their starting point. Recovering from that same forty percent loss actually requires roughly a sixty-seven percent gain just to break even.

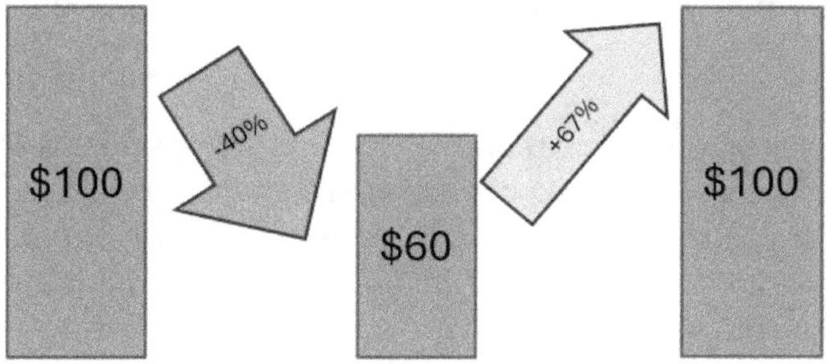

Blackjack Dicky: Retirement and Withdrawals

Blackjack Dicky retired at age seventy on December 29, 2006, with $100 in his account. That day he took his first annual withdrawal of $5, leaving $95 invested to fund his future spending.

The timing could not have been worse. Within two years, the Global Financial Crisis would cut the market nearly in half. By the end of 2008, Dicky's $95 had become $52.45, after his third withdrawal. In a single year, the market had erased almost a decade's worth of planned distributions.

At that point, the decisions became painfully real. If he keeps withdrawing $5 a year and markets stagnate, he runs out of money in about a decade. If he panics and sells at the bottom, he locks in the loss permanently and forfeits the recovery. If he cuts spending, his standard of living takes the hit instead.

For retirees, "stay the course" is easy to say and much harder to live with. Bills still have to be paid.

Dicky chose to stay invested and continue withdrawing. As a serious card player, he understands probability, volatility, and risk. He knows the worst hand at the table is not necessarily a bad hand. It is a bad hand played badly.

Early Decision Rule:
Sequence risk does not care about averages. It cares about timing.

Sequence risk does not begin on the day retirement starts. A 20 percent decline a year or two before retirement can be just as damaging. It can force delaying retirement, returning to work, or lowering the planned standard of living. That kind of hit is emotional as well as financial.

Volatility Cuts Both Ways: The Cost of Missing the Recovery

Selling in a downturn is painful. Missing the recovery can be even more damaging.

The largest recoveries are often born from the ugliest declines. Those advances rarely feel obvious while they unfold.

The dot-com bust illustrates this. The S&P 500 declined roughly 49 percent between 2000 and 2002. Recovering from that loss required nearly a one hundred percent gain. The subsequent credit and housing expansion from 2002 to 2007 delivered a one hundred percent rally, meaning that, from bust to boom, the market barely recovered to its prior peak.

S&P 500 Significant Recoveries, 1997–2026

Trough	Recovery Period	Next Peak	Recovery
Oct 1997	Post-Asian Crisis Recovery	Jul 1998	**+36%**
Aug 1998	Post-LTCM / Dot-Com Boom	Mar 2000	**+60%**
Oct 2002	Credit & Housing Expansion	Oct 2007	**+100%**
Mar 2009	Post-GFC Recovery Rally	Apr 2010	**+79%**
Jul 2010	QE2 / Risk-On Advance	Apr 2011	**+34%**
Oct 2011	Post-Eurozone Stabilization Bull	May 2015	**+94%**
Feb 2016	Post-China / Oil Recovery	Jan 2018	**+57%**
Apr 2018	Mid-Cycle Rebound	Sep 2018	**+14%**
Dec 2018	Powell Pivot Expansion	Feb 2020	**+44%**
Mar 2020	Pandemic Liquidity Boom	Jan 2022	**+114%**
Oct 2022	Post-Inflation Recovery	Feb 2023	**+17%**
Mar 2023	Post-Banking Crisis Bull Advance	Feb 2025	**+59%**

Footnote: Source: SPY ETF closing prices (price return only; dividends excluded). Dates and percentage changes are illustrative and reflect index-level moves, not client performance. Indexes are unmanaged and cannot be invested in directly. This is not a guarantee of results. See Regulatory Disclaimer / Appendix Disclosures.

Rule Extracted:
Portfolios underperform not because markets fail to recover, but because investors are no longer invested when recovery occurs.

Revisiting Blackjack Dicky

Ten years after Dicky retired, the results were clear.

On December 30, 2016, the last trading day after his eleventh annual withdrawal, Dicky's account stood at $72.27. He had taken eleven withdrawals of $5 each, the first on his first day of retirement, and one at year-end each year through 2016, totaling $55. His invested balance of $95 had still not fully recovered a decade later. He was still $22.73 below his original invested amount.

The table shows every year of Dicky's journey, the market return, the dollar gain or loss on his balance, his annual $5 withdrawal, and what remained at year's end.

Dicky's Retirement Account 2006-2016

Year	Year-End Date	Start Balance	SPY Return	$ Gain/Loss	Withdrawal	End Balance
2006	Dec 29, 2006	$100.00	—	—	$5.00	$95.00
2007	Dec 31, 2007	$95.00	+3.2%	+$3.08	$5.00	$93.08
2008	Dec 31, 2008	$93.08	**-38.3%**	**-$35.63**	$5.00	**$52.45**
2009	Dec 31, 2009	$52.45	+23.5%	+$12.32	$5.00	$59.77
2010	Dec 31, 2010	$59.77	+12.8%	+$7.67	$5.00	$62.44
2011	Dec 30, 2011	$62.44	-0.2%	-$0.12	$5.00	$57.32
2012	Dec 31, 2012	$57.32	+13.5%	+$7.72	$5.00	$60.04
2013	Dec 31, 2013	$60.04	+29.7%	+$17.83	$5.00	$72.87
2014	Dec 31, 2014	$72.87	+11.3%	+$8.23	$5.00	$76.10

Year	Year-End Date	Start Balance	SPY Return	$ Gain/Loss	Withdrawal	End Balance
2015	Dec 31, 2015	$76.10	-0.8%	-$0.62	$5.00	$70.48
2016	Dec 30, 2016	$70.48	+9.6%	+$6.80	$5.00	$72.27

Footnote: This example is for illustration only and is hypothetical. Returns are based on SPY ETF closing prices (price return only; dividends excluded) and do not reflect fees, taxes, transaction costs, or real-world implementation constraints. Results will differ for individual investors. This is not a guarantee of outcomes. See Regulatory Disclaimer / Appendix Disclosures.

The lesson is that sequence matters more than average return. Staying invested does not erase the problem when losses arrive early and withdrawals continue. Despite a strong market recovery from 2008 onward, Dicky's portfolio balance never recovered to his initial balance of $100. Early losses hit when his balance was largest, and each withdrawal came from a depleted base.

In an alternate scenario, if Dicky had retired at the end of 2008, he would have entered the market at the lows. Withdrawals would have been taken as the market rallied. The same investor, same market, but a different sequence of returns leads to a very different outcome. That is sequence risk.

Prudence: The Other Way Plans Break

Blackjack Dicky's problem was timing. Prudence's problem was temperament.

Prudence retired the same year as Dicky. She held the same portfolio and withdrew the same amount each year. She was neither reckless nor uninformed. What her plan failed to account for was temperament. She knew, even if the plan did not, that watching her balance fall 38 percent in a single year was more than she could sit through.

Her self-assessment was right. Her response was costly.

In early 2009, with her balance down sharply and no clear bottom in sight, Prudence moved to safety. She sold her position, preserved what remained in cash, and told herself she'd get back in when things stabilized. The headlines were grim. Every week brought a new reason to wait.

The market bottomed in March 2009 and began one of the strongest recoveries in modern history. Prudence missed most of it. By the time she felt comfortable re-entering, the recovery had been underway for over a year. The capital she had protected in cash never caught up.

She ended the decade worse than Dicky, not because the market treated her differently, but because her plan had been designed for someone with more tolerance than she had.

Rule Extracted:
Volatility can damage plans in two separate ways. Dicky shows what bad timing does to a disciplined investor. Prudence shows what bad structure does to an ordinary one. Dicky's outcome was hard to prevent. Prudence's was easier to mitigate. Her plan needed to be constructed for who she was.

The Planning Problem

- Volatility is the trigger; investor behavior often causes the lasting damage.
- Plans break when decisions shift from rules to reactions.
- Discipline alone is not a plan.

The capstone at the end of this act returns to Prudence and introduces a different investment strategy that would have changed the decision that cost her the recovery.

Why Diversification Alone Is Not the Answer

The conventional response to volatility is diversification. Add bonds. Invest across asset classes. Reduce concentration. That approach is widely implemented. However, the cost of that safety is often underestimated.

Assume equities have a long-term average return of ten percent annually and bonds return four percent.

- A seventy-five percent equity / twenty-five percent bond portfolio might be expected to average approximately 8.5 percent annually.
- A fifty percent equity / fifty percent bond portfolio might be expected to average approximately 7 percent annually.

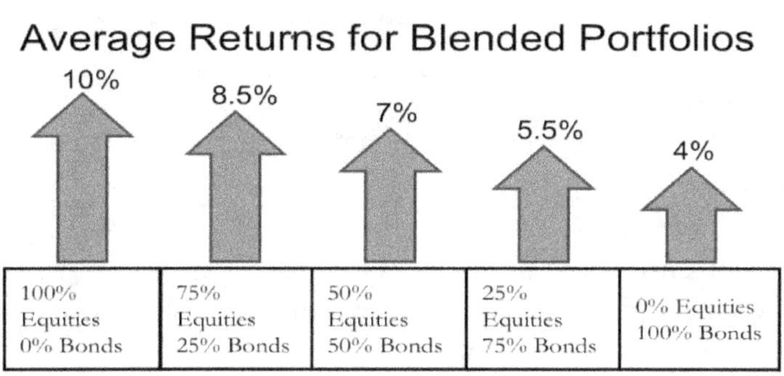

In a year when equities fall twenty percent, and bonds return four percent:

- The seventy-five/twenty-five portfolio declines roughly 14 percent.
- The fifty/fifty portfolio declines roughly 8 percent.

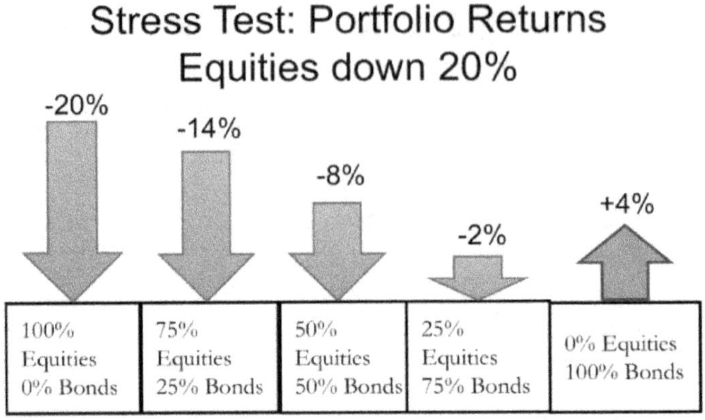

The math is straightforward. Investor behavior is harder to predict. Will a 14 percent decline trigger a change in the investor's behavior? If so, the strategy is misaligned.

> **What This Means for You:**
> If expected volatility changes behavior, the strategy is not appropriate.

Fragility does not show up in average returns. It appears when declining balances drive decisions. A retirement plan has to work in real life, not on a spreadsheet.

When Diversification Breaks: What Actually Happens During Stress

Diversification works by spreading capital across enough holdings that one company's failure does not take down the portfolio. That is the risk it was designed to solve. It was never designed to contain systemic drawdowns, when a single force pushes everything in the same direction.

A credit crisis, an inflation shock, a liquidity freeze, or a policy disruption can each become the single force that drives the market. When that happens, assets move in the same direction. Three recent crises illustrate the pattern.

Balance-Sheet Shocks (2007–2009). During the Global Financial Crisis, equities collapsed, credit markets seized, and real estate prices fell sharply. Nearly all risk assets were tied to the same constraint: funding and solvency. U.S. Treasury bonds rallied, not because bonds are inherently protective, but because interest rates collapsed as growth expectations imploded. The hedge worked because the shock was deflationary, not because diversification works universally in every crisis.

Rate Shocks (2022). Inflation surged and central banks tightened aggressively. As yields increased, bond prices fell at the same time equities declined, undermining the reliable offset from 2007-2009. In 2022, a seventy-five/twenty-five portfolio, the same allocation that mitigated losses during the Global Financial Crisis, lost far more than investors expected from a portfolio built to feel balanced.

Liquidity Shocks (2020). In early 2020, assets that normally diversify briefly moved together as investors sold what they could, not what they wanted. Even Treasuries experienced short-term selling before central bank intervention restored liquidity.

What percentage of the portfolio would need to be in bonds to prevent behavioral damage? And would that allocation still fund the retirement?

Design Choice Checkpoint:
When markets rise, strategy gets credit.
When markets fall, unexpected events get blamed.
The market does not own your outcome.
Your design choice does.

When diversified portfolios fall more than expected, or assets assumed to offset one another decline together, the question shifts from "How much am I down?" to "Is this plan broken?"

Behavior may trigger changes, from an assumed safe allocation to an even more conservative one, thus making the original retirement goals more difficult to attain.

> **Rule Extracted:**
> Diversification solves idiosyncratic risk. It does not solve systemic risk. Assigning it both jobs leaves the plan exposed.

Certainty cannot be engineered, but safeguards can be incorporated into a retirement plan. Market exposure has to be shaped intentionally so drawdowns are constrained. Poor decisions made under stress are less likely and less damaging when crises arrive.

Ask Your Advisor Today – Volatility, Behavior, and Diversification

Behavior under stress: If markets fell thirty percent tomorrow, what would this plan expect me to do, and what is built into it to reduce the chance of a bad decision?

Sequence risk: If a twenty to thirty percent decline happens within two years of retirement, what changes first: my retirement date, my spending, or my portfolio design?

Evidence, not labels: Which holdings are expected to hold value in a rate shock (2022) versus a deflationary shock (2008)? If my portfolio was permanently allocated to survive each, how would it have performed during the market recoveries and the long-term?

Chapter 2: Constructing Portfolios with Protection

There is a difference between diversification by ownership and diversification by design. Ownership means spreading capital across more funds, more asset classes, and more labels. Design means engineering exposures that behave differently in specific stress conditions. The first approach assumes assets will move independently. The second approach does not rely on that assumption.

Behavior Is a Constraint, Not a Variable

If you lived through 2008 or 2022, you have probably wondered whether there is a way to stay invested near retirement without taking the full hit. There is, but it requires a tradeoff.

Most investors hold open-ended market exposure. If the market falls thirty percent, the account falls thirty percent. No rules govern how losses and gains are treated along the way. That works when the investor has time to recover and no need to withdraw. It works poorly when losses arrive early in retirement, withdrawals are already underway, and a thirty-eight percent decline no longer feels temporary.

> **Reality Check:**
> Discipline is not a risk-control system.

Investments with contractual rules that set the boundaries for gains and losses in advance give a portfolio the discipline that the investor cannot guarantee otherwise. The terms are fixed at the start and do not change with markets or headlines.

Early Decision Rule:
These strategies reduce the exposure to the worst outcomes in exchange for less participation in the best ones. The trade-offs need to be recognized and understood to determine if the strategy is right for the investor.

Protection: Buffers, Floors, and Barriers

These are the structures that would have changed Prudence's outcome. Each one defines how loss is absorbed before it reaches the investor.

A **buffer** absorbs the initial losses over the period. If the buffer is fifteen percent, the first fifteen percent decline is absorbed. A ten percent decline produces roughly zero percent return. A twenty percent decline produces roughly a five percent loss, the portion beyond the buffer.

In 2008, the S&P 500 fell 38.3 percent. With a fifteen percent buffer, that decline becomes approximately 23.3 percent. Still painful, but survivable. A 23.3 percent loss is a bad year. A 38.3 percent loss is the kind of hit that forces a retiree to cut risk or abandon the plan. Buffers are designed to make common corrections survivable, not to eliminate large losses entirely.

A **floor** works in reverse. The investor absorbs the initial losses. Everything beyond the floor is absorbed by the structure. Whether the index ends down fifteen percent or thirty-five percent, the loss is limited to the floor.

In 2008, a ten percent floor meant a ten percent loss while the market lost thirty-eight percent. The floor does not eliminate risk. It defines the boundary. When the worst case is known in advance, behavior becomes more reliable.

A barrier is conditional protection. Barriers are typically set at seventy to seventy-five percent of the starting value. At maturity, if the asset finishes above the barrier, the full principal is returned regardless of what happened in between. If the asset finishes below the barrier, the protection disappears entirely and losses are realized as if the index had been owned outright.

In 2008, a structure with a seventy percent barrier would have lost approximately thirty-eight percent, matching the market. If the same asset had finished down twenty-nine percent instead, the structure would have returned one hundred percent of the original investment.

Each structure answers a different behavioral question.
Buffers fit investors who can tolerate some loss but want common drawdowns softened.
Floors fit investors who need a hard limit on how bad a defined period can become.
Barriers fit investors willing to accept a binary outcome in exchange for richer upside terms.

> **Reality Check:**
> A barrier is a conditional promise, not guaranteed protection. The investor owns the full downside risk if conditions fail.

What Protection Costs

Protection is not free. The price is usually reflected in the upside terms.

The most common expression of the tradeoff is a **cap**. A cap is the maximum gain that can be earned at maturity. If the cap is fourteen percent and the asset rises thirty percent, the gain is fourteen percent. The cap might seem restrictive, but it is the cost of the protection.

In 2009, the S&P 500 recovered 23.5 percent. An investor with a fourteen percent cap would have captured fourteen percent. Short of the full rebound, but real participation. Sacrificing 9.5

percentage points of upside in 2009 to absorb fifteen fewer percentage points of loss in 2008 is a trade most retirees would make every time.

A damaged plan does not recover by switching to a more conservative allocation. It recovers by not taking the full hit in the first place. The contractual terms exist to prevent that damage, independent of asset performance.

Some structures use what is called a participation rate, sharing a percentage of the gain instead of capping it. This can offer more upside in exchange for less protection or longer holding periods.

Two questions decide whether a structure belongs in the plan. Does the protection change behavior in a bad sequence? Is the remaining upside still acceptable for the long-term plan? If either answer is no, the structure is wrong, regardless of how attractive it looks on a payoff chart.

Design Choice Checkpoint:
The difference between buffers, floors, and barriers is a deliberate choice, whether protection needs to be dependable or conditionality is acceptable.

Once established, the contractual rules that determine how outcomes are measured, how losses are calculated, and what upside is surrendered cannot change. Headlines and contagion impact asset values, not the terms of the contract.

Additional structures, including step-up designs that address flat and mildly negative markets, additional payoff variations and blended combinations are detailed in the Appendix for readers who want the full mechanical picture.

Chapter 3 shows where these tools fit inside a portfolio and how they compare to bonds.

Ask Your Advisor Today – Constructing Portfolios with Protection

Behavioral Fit: Which strategy best fits my temperament, and what impact would it have on my portfolio during the 2008 and 2022 shocks as well as the strong recovery years that followed?
Stress test: In a 2008-style year, how does adding this defined-outcome layer change my expected overall drawdown?

Chapter 3: A Designed Portfolio in Action

Chapter 2 introduced the protection mechanisms: buffers, floors, and barriers. This chapter shows where they belong inside a portfolio, what job each one does, and why they are not a replacement for bonds but a different tool entirely.

> **Early Decision Rule:**
> Defined-outcome structures exist to keep investors invested through the conditions that force most of them out. Beating the market was never the job.

Where Designed Outcomes Fit in the Portfolio

Designed strategies separate capital by function rather than spreading it across more labels.

- Liquidity capital protects near-term spending.
- Stability capital limits drawdowns and supports behavior.
- Growth capital compounds over the long term.

Most designed-outcome structures belong in the stability layer. When drawdowns are contained, growth capital can stay invested and compound without interruption.

Anita and the Stability Layer
Anita is sixty-three and recently retired. She allocates $500,000 to a one-year strategy tied to a U.S. equity index with a fifteen percent buffer and a fourteen percent cap.

In 2022, the S&P 500 fell 19.5 percent. Without the buffer, $500,000 becomes $402,600. Anita's buffer strategy absorbed the first fifteen percent loss and ended the year at $477,500. In 2023, the index recovered 24.3 percent. The non-buffered investment recovers to $500,400, roughly back to even after two years.

Anita's buffered strategy is capped at fourteen percent and grows to $544,350.

A 19.5 percent decline followed by a 24.3 percent gain, would seem to produce a clear net gain. Mathematically, it barely recovered to even. Anita's buffered strategy finished with a higher balance because smaller losses need smaller recoveries.

At the end of 2022, one investor's balance is $402,600 and the other's is $477,500. The first one may question the plan. The second one does not. The buffer did not change the market. It changed the decision.

> **What This Means for You:**
> Winning every year is not the objective. The goal is structural, to prevent one bad year from forcing a permanent decision.

If a market downturn lasts for several years, the strategy resets at maturity and a new period begins. Each period measures only the change in the index from its new starting point. Last year's decline is irrelevant.

Stability Capital: Defined Outcomes vs. Bonds

A natural question follows. If designed-outcome structures provide stability, why not just use bonds?

Bonds generate income and support near-term cash needs. They can be sold any day without a surrender penalty or a maturity constraint. For liquidity capital, bonds are the right tool. For stability capital, bonds depend on a correlation assumption: that they rise or remain unchanged when stocks fall. In 2022, the Federal Reserve raised rates at the fastest pace in forty years. Bonds fell sharply in the same year equities declined.

Defined-outcome structures do not depend on that assumption. The protection is contractual, not correlational. Typically, the return potential is higher. A fourteen percent cap offers more upside than a bond portfolio yielding four to five percent.

The tradeoff is liquidity. Bonds can be sold tomorrow. Defined-outcome structures are designed to be held to maturity. Early exit may produce a result that does not match the maturity payoff.

A well-engineered plan uses both. Bonds for liquidity and income. Designed outcomes for behavioral durability and higher return potential over defined periods. They are complements, not substitutes.

Opportunity: Structured Growth with Real Trade-Offs

Growth-oriented structured notes combine a contingent barrier with a participation multiplier that amplifies gains.

Hank and the 2008 Opportunity
The S&P 500 ended 2008 at 90.24. Hank had $2 million in liquid assets, of which $400,000 was earning almost nothing in a money market fund as rates were near zero. He wanted to participate in a recovery, but not without some protection after a thirty-eight percent decline.

He invested half of the $400,000 in a three-year growth note on the last day of the year tied to the S&P 500 with a twenty percent barrier and a 1.25 participation multiplier. The barrier sat at approximately 72, eighty percent of the initial level. The index would need to close below that level three years later for the protection to fail.

The S&P 500 ended 2011 at 125.50, a gain of roughly 39 percent. The 1.25 multiplier produced a return of approximately 49 percent. Hank's $200,000 became approximately $298,000. His other $200,000, left in a money market for three years, was still roughly $200,000.

Hank was not trying to time the market. He was looking at the math. If the S&P 500 fell anywhere from zero to twenty percent over the next three years, the barrier held and he got his full principal back, and the return would slightly lag the performance of the money market fund. If the market recovered at all, the multiplier amplified the gain. If the barrier broke, losses would be realized from the starting point. The barrier and the multiplier did not eliminate risk. They reframed the risk-reward context of the investment.

Protection, Control, and Opportunity, By Design
Three tools. Three jobs. One system.

Job	Typical tools	Purpose in the plan
Protection	Buffers, Floors	Blunt bad sequences when retirement is vulnerable
Control	Defined-outcome income and stability structures	Compress middling outcomes so the plan remains usable
Opportunity	Growth notes	Pursue upside without risking essential spending

Protection and control belong in stability capital. Opportunity belongs in a small, defined allocation within growth capital. The effectiveness of these investments is based on the likelihood of the investor staying invested and remaining able to meet the retirement plan's goals through the kind of markets reality delivers. A plan that requires structured notes to be liquidity capital is an over-engineered plan.

Ask Your Advisor Today – A Designed Portfolio in Action
Portfolio Design: What in my portfolio serves the protection role, what serves the control role, and what serves the opportunity role?
Capital Allocation: How is my capital divided between liquidity, stability, and growth, and what is each bucket designed to do when markets fall?

Integration Check: Act I Volatility and Portfolio Design

1. What is the maximum drawdown my plan is designed to tolerate? What specifically changes at declines of ten, twenty, and thirty percent?
2. In a systemic shock, which holdings are expected to hold value? Is there an order in which assets are liquidated if cash is needed?
3. How are designed-outcome structures integrated into the portfolio? What changes to open-ended exposure are made when they are included?
4. Are defined-outcome strategies placed in the accounts where their tax and liquidity characteristics are most efficient?

Readers who want full engineering details, including additional payoff structures, blended strategies, delivery vehicles, and governance frameworks will find it in the Appendix.

ACT I CAPSTONE: Prudence's Real Choice, What Defined Outcomes Are Actually For

Blackjack Dicky survived. He retired into the worst possible sequence, stayed invested through a thirty-eight percent loss, and ended a decade later still in the game. Prudence could not do that. Her plan was built for a Dicky, and she was a Prudence. Act I identified the behavioral problem. This capstone tests the structural answer.

What If the Plan Had Been Built for Prudence?

Assume Prudence had entered retirement in the buffered/cap strategy described in Chapters 2 and 3: a fifteen percent buffer and a fourteen percent annual cap, reset each year. Same starting balance. Same $5 annual withdrawal. Same dates.

Year	Year-End Date	SPY Return	Buffered Strategy Return	Gain/ Loss	With-drawal	Prudence End Balance	Dicky End Balance
2006	Dec 29, 2006	—	—	—	$5.00	**$95.00**	$95.00
2007	Dec 31, 2007	+3.2%	+3.2%	+$3.08	$5.00	**$93.08**	$93.08
2008	Dec 31, 2008	**-38.3%**	**-23.3% ‡**	**-$21.67**	$5.00	**$66.41**	**$52.45**
2009	Dec 31, 2009	+23.5%	*+14.0% **	+$9.30	$5.00	**$70.71**	$59.77
2010	Dec 31, 2010	+12.8%	+12.8%	+$9.07	$5.00	**$74.78**	$62.44
2011	Dec 30, 2011	**-0.2%**	**0.0% †**	+$0.00	$5.00	**$69.78**	$57.32
2012	Dec 31, 2012	+13.5%	+13.5%	+$9.40	$5.00	**$74.18**	$60.04
2013	Dec 31, 2013	+29.7%	*+14.0% **	+$10.39	$5.00	**$79.57**	$72.87

Year	Year-End Date	SPY Return	Buffered Strategy Return	Gain/ Loss	With-drawal	Prudence End Balance	Dicky End Balance
2014	Dec 31, 2014	+11.3%	+11.3%	+$8.99	$5.00	**$83.55**	$76.10
2015	Dec 31, 2015	**-0.8%**	**0.0% †**	+$0.00	$5.00	**$78.55**	$70.48
2016	Dec 30, 2016	+9.6%	+9.6%	+$7.58	$5.00	**$81.13**	**$72.27**

$100 starting balance | $5 annual withdrawal | 15% buffer | 14% annual cap | Assumes annual reset into the same terms at each year-end measurement.

* Capped, market gain exceeded 14% cap: excess forfeited

† Fully buffered, loss absorbed entirely by 15% buffer

‡ Partial buffer, loss exceeds 15%; losses beyond buffer absorbed by investor.

The number that matters most is 2008. The 38.3 percent market decline that hit Dicky's portfolio directly became approximately 23.3 percent for Prudence. Her balance fell from $93.08 to $66.41 instead of $52.45. She still lost ground, but she did not lose the plan.

A 38.3 percent loss in a single year and a 23.3 percent loss are not the same experience. One can look like collapse. The other is survivable. For an investor like Prudence, that gap is what separates staying invested from stopping out.

By the end of 2016, Prudence's balance stands at $81.13 versus Dicky's $72.27, a difference of $8.86, or 12.3 percent, even though her gains were capped in three of the eleven years shown.

The Honest Counterargument

This comparison covers exactly the kind of environment buffers are designed to address: a severe early drawdown. That context matters and should be stated plainly.

Reset the clock to December 31, 2008, the bottom. If Prudence had entered the same structure at the lows instead of the highs, the buffer would have provided little benefit because the major loss had already happened. From 2009 through 2016, Dicky's open-ended equity exposure returned 38 percent, while Prudence's capped structure returned 22 percent. The cap's cost is real. In a sustained bull market with few corrections, a defined-outcome structure is often the more expensive choice. Any comparison that does not show that is selling something.

The planning decision is which structure is more likely to keep this investor invested through the conditions she is actually likely to face.

Prudence's Real Choice

Here is what the table cannot show: Prudence's actual decision.

She did not choose between $81.13 and $72.27. She chose between a structure that might have kept her invested and the actual path she followed, stopping out, sitting in cash through the recovery, and re-entering too late. That outcome was worse than either figure in the comparison. Unlike the cap's cost, it was permanent. Capital that exits near the bottom and misses the recovery does not simply reappear.

The buffer did not make Prudence a better investor. It made the plan more compatible with the investor she actually was. That is the most important point.

A theoretically superior strategy that gets abandoned in the middle of a decline is not superior in practice. The best strategy for Prudence was never the one with the highest expected return. It was the one she could stay with when the market gave her every reason to leave.

> **Rule Extracted:**
> A plan you can stay with will outperform a plan you cannot, regardless of how it looks on paper.

What This Act Was About

The chapters in this act had one objective: making sure an investor like Prudence can survive a temporary decline without making a permanent decision.

Defined outcomes are not designed to beat the market or eliminate volatility. They are tools for shaping what happens when markets misbehave so the investor can stay invested long enough for the plan to work.

Market downturns can happen quickly. Tax damage builds more slowly and often goes unnoticed until the options are gone. A portfolio can produce strong gross returns and still deliver disappointing spendable income when withdrawals are taken from the wrong accounts at the wrong time. Act II is where the fortress becomes more concrete: not by changing markets, but by changing what the tax code gets to claim.

Ask Your Advisor Today – Prudence Capstone
Behavioral fit: Given my actual tolerance, not my theoretical one, is my current portfolio structured for the investor I am or the investor I wish I were?
Structural protection: If markets dropped twenty-five percent in the first two years of retirement, what specific feature of my plan would reduce the chance of the decision that cost Prudence the recovery?

Table Footnote: Illustration only. Returns shown are based on SPY price returns (dividends excluded) and simplified buffer/cap assumptions. Actual contract terms, fees, surrender charges, taxes, and crediting methods can change results. Indexes are unmanaged and cannot be invested in directly. This is not a guarantee of outcomes. See Regulatory Disclaimer / Appendix Disclosures.

ACT II: The Tax System and Retirement Assets

Market volatility arrives suddenly. A portfolio drops thirty percent, and the damage is visible the same day. Taxes operate differently. They build slowly, almost invisibly, compounding across years of uncoordinated decisions until the consequences arrive all at once.

The accumulation phase masks the problem. Pre-tax contributions feel painless. Balances grow without a visible cost. The IRA swells. Nobody sends a statement showing what the government's share will be when withdrawals begin.

Once retirement starts, the bill arrives. Required minimum distributions push dollars into income whether the household needs them or not. Each additional dollar can classify a larger portion of Social Security as taxable, increase Medicare premiums, and cost a surviving spouse even more through a narrower bracket structure. The conversion windows that could have softened the damage do not stay open forever.

This act maps the tax system, the retirement account landscape, and the interaction between Social Security, Medicare, and income. It outlines those interactions so that no decision is made without understanding what it triggers and how it affects the retirement plan.

Chapter 4: How Taxes Work and Where the Damage Hides

> **Early Decision Rule:**
> You do not control the tax code. You control how exposed your plan is to it. Exposure is a design choice, and much of it is determined long before the tax planning conversation begins.

Tax consequences are shaped over many years by how money was saved, invested, and spent. Two investors can save the same amount, earn the same returns, and retire with very different after-tax wealth. What separates them is whether taxes were integrated into the plan from the start or left to the annual tax return.

> **Reality Check:**
> If your tax planning starts when you file your tax return, you are not planning. You are documenting.

How the Tax System Actually Works

Taxes are calculated based on three factors: character, timing, and rate. Most mistakes are not exotic. They come from not understanding how these three factors interact: what type of income is being created, when it is being triggered, and what the tax on the next dollar will be.

Not all income is taxed the same way. At the federal level, the two most common categories are ordinary income and long-term capital gains. Ordinary income includes wages, interest, short-term gains, and withdrawals from traditional IRAs and 401(k)s. It is taxed at higher rates. Long-term capital gains and qualified dividends are taxed at preferential rates. What separates the two is the holding period: a long-term capital gain is profit from selling an asset held longer than one year.

Paper gains do not create current tax. The trigger is activity: earning, selling, or withdrawing. The gap between what has grown and what has been realized is one of the most powerful levers in retirement planning.

Brackets and Marginal Rates

The federal income tax system is progressive. Income is taxed in layers, not all at one rate. The first dollars of taxable income are taxed at ten percent. As income rises, each additional layer is taxed at the next bracket rate. A household in the thirty-two percent bracket pays that rate only on the dollars that fall within it. Everything below is taxed at the lower rates that came before it.

Current Federal Income Tax Brackets

Marginal Rate	Single Filers	Married Filing Jointly
10%	Up to $12,400	Up to $24,800
12%	$12,401 – $50,400	$24,801 – $100,800
22%	$50,401 – $105,700	$100,801 – $211,400
24%	$105,701 – $201,775	$211,401 – $403,550
32%	$201,776 – $256,225	$403,551 – $512,450
35%	$256,226 – $640,600	$512,451 – $768,700
37%	Over $640,600	Over $768,700

Source: IRS inflation adjustments for tax year 2026 (Rev. Proc. 2025-32 / IR-2025-103). Figures apply to taxable income for tax year 2026 (returns filed in 2027) and may change in future years.

Current Federal Long Term Capital Gains Tax Rates

Rate	Single Filers	Married Filing Jointly
0%	Up to $49,450	Up to $98,900
15%	$49,451 – $545,500	$98,901 – $613,700
20%	Over $545,500	Over $613,700

Source: IRS inflation adjustments for 2026 capital gains thresholds (Rev. Proc. 2025-32).

Additional Layers

The federal bracket is only part of the bill. Most states impose their own income tax on top. Some cities add a local tax as well. Combined federal, state, and local marginal rates on ordinary income can be substantial, and they vary significantly by where you live. A retiree in Florida faces a very different effective rate than one in New York or California.

Higher-income households face a 3.8 percent surcharge on net investment income when modified adjusted gross income exceeds $200,000 (single) or $250,000 (joint). It does not appear in the bracket tables, but it raises the effective rate on investment dollars once the income threshold is crossed.

Beyond the Bracket: Thresholds

Not all tax costs are gradual. Brackets are progressive, each dollar taxed a little more than the last. Thresholds work differently. They are cliffs. One dollar over the line and a fixed surcharge or tax event is triggered.

Medicare premiums and Social Security taxation both operate this way. A single withdrawal, conversion, or asset sale that crosses one of these lines can cost far more than the bracket rate would suggest. Chapter 6 maps these interactions in detail.

The full cost of the next dollar is often higher than the bracket alone.

Deductions and Itemizing: What Matters for Planning

Taxable income is income after adjustments and deductions, not the gross number on a pay stub.

Before rates are applied, the taxpayer reduces taxable income by choosing the more favorable of two deduction methods:

- Standard deduction: a fixed amount set by the IRS that reduces taxable income automatically
- Itemized deductions: specific qualifying expenses: state and local taxes (subject to caps), mortgage interest, and charitable contributions

Itemized deductions only create additional tax benefit once total deductible expenses exceed the standard baseline.

How and when dollars leave the household matters as much as what comes in. Charitable giving is the clearest example of how structure changes the tax result even when the amount given stays the same.

Strategic Giving: Tax-Efficient Charitable Planning

The deduction framework creates its own dynamic when applied to charitable giving. Dollars that would otherwise go to taxes can be redirected toward causes you actually care about.

> **Early Decision Rule:**
> The same dollar, given from the wrong account at the wrong time, can cost the donor more in taxes and deliver less to the charity.

Qualified Charitable Distributions: A QCD allows an individual age 70½ or older to direct IRA funds to a qualified charity. The distribution is excluded from taxable income and can count toward the year's required minimum distribution, which can help manage Social Security taxation and IRMAA thresholds.

Donating Appreciated Securities: JoJo owns $100,000 of stock originally purchased for $25,000. If JoJo sells the stock first, the $75,000 gain creates capital gains tax and reduces what is left to give. Instead, if JoJo donates the shares directly to a qualified charity, the capital gain is never realized, and the charity receives the full market value. His generosity does not change. The tax cost does.

	Sell Stock, Then Donate	Donate Stock Directly
Original cost basis	$25,000	$25,000
Current market value	$100,000	$100,000
Capital gain	$75,000	$75,000
Capital gains tax (25%)	$18,750	$0
Net benefit to charity	$81,250	$100,000
Tax deduction benefit	**$30,875**	**$38,000**
Charity receives more		**+$18,750**
JoJo's larger deduction		**+$7,125**

Table Footnote: Simplified illustration using assumed rates (25% capital gains; 38% combined marginal rate = 32% federal + 6% state). Actual rates depend on income, state, deductions, and NIIT.

The same generosity, structured differently, produces a measurably better result.

Donor-Advised Funds: A donor-advised fund allows a donor to make an irrevocable contribution of appreciated assets and receive an immediate tax deduction. Grants to charities can be made over time, separating the tax deduction from the giving itself. The deduction can be taken when it creates the most value, specifically in unusually high-income years.

The goal is to make generosity more effective and fully coordinated with the broader income plan. Charitable structure is one lever. Filing status is another, and its impact is often larger and not anticipated.

Toby's Tax Shock

Toby spent fifteen years on the professional bowling circuit, earning $400,000 a year from tournament winnings and shoe endorsements. Toby was meticulous about lane conditions, ball weight, and release angle. Tax planning was a different story.

When the divorce became final and the filing status changed, Toby did not expect a $29,666 tax increase. Not one additional dollar was earned.

At $400,000 of income as married filing jointly, the $32,200 standard deduction reduces taxable income to $367,800. Federal tax liability is approximately $73,468. The marginal tax rate is twenty-four percent, and the effective rate is about 18.4 percent.

After the divorce, as a single filer, the standard deduction falls to $16,100. Toby's marginal rate jumps to thirty-two percent, and the federal tax bill rises to approximately $103,134, an effective rate of 25.8 percent.

That is $29,666 more in federal tax in a single year, more than a forty percent increase, without earning an additional dollar.

	Married Filing Jointly	Single (after the divorce)
Annual Income	$400,000	$400,000
Standard Deduction	$32,200	$16,100
Taxable Income	$367,800	$383,900
Federal Income Tax	$73,468	$103,134
Marginal Tax Rate	24%	32%
Effective Tax Rate	18.4%	25.8%

Table Footnote: Simplified illustration using 2026 federal brackets and standard deduction only. Does not model itemized deductions, credits, payroll taxes, IRMAA, state tax, or other adjustments. Approximate results.

Filing status is not an administrative detail. It is a bracket change with a five-figure annual consequence.

The Widow/Widower's Penalty: Minnie and Jean

The same filing-status compression that surprised Toby appears in a more common and more devastating form: widowhood.

Jean and Minnie are retired with $300,000 in combined annual income: $80,000 from Social Security, $80,000 from a pension, and $140,000 in required minimum distributions. Filing jointly, they claim the $32,200 standard deduction, and 85% of their Social Security is taxable at that income level. Their taxable income is $255,800, placing them in the twenty-four percent marginal bracket. The federal tax bill is approximately $46,588, an effective rate of about 15.5 percent, leaving $253,412 in after-tax spendable income.

When one spouse dies, household income drops immediately. Social Security falls to the higher of the two benefits, which in this example reduces it to $40,000. The pension continues. The IRA distributions continue on the same schedule. Gross income falls from $300,000 to $260,000.

The surviving spouse now files as a single taxpayer. Everything changes.

	Both Spouses (MFJ)	Surviving Spouse (Single)
Social Security	$80,000	$40,000
Pension	$80,000	$80,000
RMD	$140,000	$140,000
Gross Income	$300,000	$260,000
Standard Deduction	$32,200	$16,100
Taxable Income	$255,800	$237,900
Marginal Bracket	24%	32%
Federal Tax	**$46,588**	**$52,584**
Effective Rate	15.5%	20.2%

	Both Spouses (MFJ)	Surviving Spouse (Single)
After-Tax Income	$253,412	$207,416

Table Footnote: Simplified illustration using 2026 federal brackets and standard deduction only. Social Security taxation is modeled at the stated income level. Does not model itemized deductions, credits, IRMAA, state tax, or other adjustments. Approximate results.

Gross income dropped $40,000. The federal tax bill went up by $5,996. The surviving spouse earns less and pays more. That is the widow's penalty. It is not a rare edge case. It is the automatic consequence of losing a spouse at this income level. The bracket compression from married filing jointly to single, combined with the reduced standard deduction, turns a $40,000 income loss into a $46,000 after-tax income loss.

The tax code does not pause for grief. It arrives when the surviving spouse is least equipped to respond.

The window to address it is while both spouses are alive. That means it belongs in the plan now, not later. Chapter 9 shows what that planning looks like in practice and what it can produce.

Ask Your Advisor Today – How Taxes Work and Where the Damage Hides

Bracket awareness: What is my current marginal bracket, what would push me into the next one, and what is the full cost of that next dollar including thresholds?

Donation priority: Based on my holdings, what is the right giving sequence this year: appreciated securities, donor-advised fund, QCD, or cash? Why?

Filing status risk: What is the tax cost of a change in filing status, whether from divorce, death, or retirement, and has it been modeled?

Chapter 5: The Retirement Account Landscape

Chapter 4 showed how income is taxed. This chapter is about where that income comes from, because the account that holds the asset determines the tax treatment when money goes in, while it grows, and when it comes out.

Account Type	Funded With	Growth	Withdrawals	RMDs
Tax-Deferred 401(k), 403(b), Traditional IRA	Pre-tax dollars	Tax-deferred	Taxed as ordinary income	Yes (age 73)
Roth, Roth IRA, Roth 401(k)	After-tax dollars	Tax-free	Tax-free (if qualified)	No (Roth IRA)
HSA Health Savings Account	Pre-tax dollars	Tax-free	Tax-free (medical expenses)	No
Alternative Vehicles 529, Insurance	After-tax dollars	Tax-deferred or tax-free	Varies by vehicle	No

Table Footnote: Summary only. Rules vary by plan and can change. RMD rules depend on birth year and account type; confirm current rules before implementing.

Container Ladder

What Each Account Type Buys You:

- Taxable brokerage: no withdrawal restrictions, capital-gains treatment, and step-up in basis for heirs.
- Tax-deferred (401(k) / IRA): deduction today, taxed later as ordinary income, and RMDs beginning at age 73.
- Roth: tax-free qualified withdrawals, no impact on brackets or IRMAA, and no RMDs.

- HSA: tax-free contributions, growth, and withdrawals for qualified medical expenses. No RMDs.
- Special-purpose vehicles (529 / insurance): goal-specific tax treatment for problems the other containers do not solve well.

Tax-Deferred Accounts (401(k), 403(b), Traditional IRA)

Tax-deferred accounts are the foundation of most retirement savings strategies. The assumption behind them is that retirement income will be lower than working income, placing the taxpayer in a lower bracket when the tax is finally paid. That assumption is not always correct, and when it is wrong, the cost can be substantial. Later chapters show when and why.

Understanding tax deferral starts with two things: what can be contributed and what the deduction is actually worth at the current marginal rate.

> **Reality Check:**
> A traditional IRA or 401(k) balance is pre-tax purchasing power, not spendable wealth. The IRS owns a share of every dollar in that account. The only question is how large that share will be when the bill comes due.

Pre-Tax Contribution Limits

The benefit of pre-tax contributions is immediate. Every dollar contributed reduces taxable income in the year it is made. For someone in the 32% bracket, that tax savings is worth 32 cents on every dollar contributed. The limits determine how much tax-advantaged space is available each year. For high earners, the gap between what can be contributed and what the plan actually needs is where strategy begins.

Current Key Retirement Contribution Limits

Item	Current limit	Notes
401(k)/403(b)/TSP employee elective deferral	$24,500	Age 50+ catch-up: +$8,000 (total $32,500). Ages 60–63 "higher catch-up": +$11,250 (total $35,750).
IRA contribution limit (Traditional + Roth combined)	$7,500	Age 50+ catch-up: +$1,100 (total $8,600).
401(k) annual additions (aggregate) limit	$72,000	Includes employee + employer + (if permitted) after-tax contributions; excludes catch-up contributions.

Source: IRS 2026 cost-of-living adjustments (IR-2025-111; Notice 2025-67).

Norma & Gertrude: The Real Cost of a 401(k) Contribution

Two single sisters are deciding whether to make pre-tax contributions to their company's 401(k). Their federal marginal rates and state tax liabilities are shown in the following table.

Item	Norma No Contrib	Norma PreTax Contrib	Gertrude No Contrib	Gertrude PreTax Contrib
Gross salary	$200,000	$200,000	$250,000	$250,000
Federal marginal rate	24%	24%	32%	32%
Pre-tax 401(k) contribution	$0	**$24,500**	$0	**$24,500**
Illustrated Taxable income (simplified)	$200,000	$175,500	$250,000	$225,500

Item	Norma No Contrib	Norma PreTax Contrib	Gertrude No Contrib	Gertrude PreTax Contrib
Federal income tax	$40,598	$34,718	$56,456	$48,616
State income tax (6%)	$12,000	$10,530	$15,000	$13,530
Total taxes paid	$52,598	$45,248	$71,456	$62,146
NET TAKE-HOME PAY	$147,402	**$130,252**	$178,544	**$163,354**
Change in take-home	-	-$17,150	-	-$15,190
401(k) dollars invested	$0	**$24,500**	$0	**$24,500**

Note: Simplified and directional only; actual taxable income and taxes depend on deductions, credits, payroll taxes, state rules, and other adjustments.

Both sisters contribute $24,500, the pre-tax maximum to their 401(k), yet their take-home pay falls by much less than the contribution amount. Norma's pay drops by only $17,150, while Gertrude's drops by $15,190. Every dollar Norma contributes costs her about 70 cents in reduced take-home pay; every dollar Gertrude contributes costs about 62 cents. The higher the bracket, the larger the subsidy.

Roth Accounts (Roth IRA, Roth 401(k)/403(b))

Where tax-deferred accounts postpone the tax bill, Roth accounts eliminate it on qualified withdrawals. From that point forward, the money belongs entirely to the retiree.

> **Reality Check:**
> Unlike a tax-deferred account, the statement balance of a Roth is its actual spendable value. No hidden tax lien. No future bracket risk. What you see is what you keep.

Roth withdrawals are not counted as taxable income, which makes them a powerful tool for controlling taxable income in retirement. The downstream effects on Social Security taxation and IRMAA are covered later in the book.

Roth 401(k) and Roth IRA contribution limits are the same as traditional pre-tax 401(k) and IRA limits. Roth IRA eligibility is subject to income limits. Many high earners cannot make direct Roth IRA contributions, but strategies to build Roth balances still exist.

Whether to prioritize pre-tax or Roth cannot be answered by limits alone. It depends on future tax rates, withdrawal sequencing, and how RMDs interact with thresholds. Later chapters show how those interactions create real costs and where planning creates advantage.

When Alternative "Retirement" Vehicles Make Sense

Retirement accounts are not the only containers worth building. Several other vehicles offer similar tax advantages or operate outside standard IRS contribution limits. Each solves a problem the others do not.

HSA: triple-tax-advantaged, best used as a long-term medical spending reserve. 529: tax-free growth for education, no RMDs. Insurance: tax-deferred growth outside IRS contribution limits. Long-term care insurance: tax-free benefits that prevent forced liquidation. Further details are in Act IV and the Appendix.

What This Means for You:
Income-producing assets in tax-deferred accounts (where interest and dividends grow without an annual tax bill), long-term growth in taxable accounts (where heirs get a step-up in basis), and highest-growth assets in Roth (where gains are never taxed).

Grandma Hannah: The Container Determines the Outcome

Hannah bought $100,000 of stock in a winter-hat company decades ago because she had worn one of their hats and thought it was the finest she had ever owned. She believed in the product, and she was right. The stock is now worth $300,000. She never focused on where she held it. That decision was made years ago, but it determines how much of the $200,000 gain her family actually keeps and how much is lost to taxes.

The investment is identical in every scenario below. The tax result is not. The container determines the outcome.

Scenario	Taxable Brokerage	Traditional IRA/401(k)	Roth IRA
Original investment	$100,000	$100,000	$100,000
Current value	$300,000	$300,000	$300,000
Gain	$200,000	$200,000	$200,000
IF GRANDMA SELLS			
Taxable amount	$200,000 (gain)	$300,000 (all)	**$0**
Tax rate	25%	25%	**0%**
Tax owed	$50,000	$75,000	**$0**
Net proceeds	**$250,000**	**$225,000**	**$300,000**
IF HEIRS INHERIT			
Heirs' cost basis	**$300,000 (stepped-up)**	**$0**	**N/A (tax-free)**
Tax if heirs sell	**$0**	$75,000	**$0**
Net proceeds to heirs	**$300,000**	**$225,000**	**$300,000**

Table Footnote: Simplified illustration using a placeholder blended tax rate to highlight structural differences (not precise bracket math). Actual rates depend on brackets, deductions, state tax, and income sources.

In the taxable account, only the gain is taxed, and heirs may eliminate that gain entirely through a step-up in basis. In the traditional IRA, the full withdrawal is taxed as ordinary income both during Hannah's life and when heirs distribute the inherited account. In the Roth, there is no tax at either point.

Asset location is a lifetime after-tax decision. Which account holds the asset determines how much of the wealth is kept and how much is lost. This is true for both the retiree and for the people who inherit the accounts.

Design Choice Checkpoint
Start with three questions:
1. Am I buying a deduction now (tax-deferred) or buying control later (Roth)?
2. Do I expect forced income later through RMDs, and can I reduce it?
3. Will I have at least two levers in retirement, taxable and tax-free, so I am not locked into one bracket?

This chapter is the map. Every account type has rules for what goes in, how it grows, and what it costs to take out. The later acts show how those rules interact with brackets, thresholds, and timing to determine how much of this wealth is actually yours to spend.

Ask Your Advisor Today – The Retirement Account Landscape
Tax trajectory: What is my projected marginal tax rate in retirement compared to today, and what drives the difference: RMDs, filing status, or both?
After-tax value: What are my current account balances actually worth after tax, and have we modeled that number?

Chapter 6: Social Security, Medicare, and the Income Tax Intersection

> **Early Decision Rule:**
> Social Security timing, Medicare premiums, and RMD withdrawals are not separate decisions. They are the same income problem viewed from three angles.

Three forces shape retirement income in ways most households never model. Social Security timing determines when benefits begin and sets the permanent income floor for the surviving spouse. Medicare premiums respond to income decisions made two years earlier. And a single additional IRA dollar can cause previously untaxed Social Security benefits to become taxable and trigger IRMAA surcharges, raising the effective cost of that dollar well above its bracket rate.

This chapter maps those interactions so that no income decision is made without understanding what it triggers.

When Distributions Trigger a Second Tax

Withdrawals from retirement accounts can trigger a secondary tax effect. As income rises, a larger portion of Social Security benefits becomes taxable, raising the effective cost of each additional dollar withdrawn.

Social Security taxation is determined by a formula known as **combined income**. For married couples filing jointly, the thresholds work as follows:

Combined Income	=	Adjusted Gross Income	+	Tax-Exempt Interest	+	½ Social Security Benefits

- Under $32,000: Social Security benefits are not taxable
- $32,000–$44,000: Up to fifty percent of benefits become taxable
- Over $44,000: Up to eighty-five percent of benefits become taxable

(Thresholds are lower for single filers.)

The claiming decision itself, when to file, how to protect the surviving spouse, and how to coordinate with Roth conversions, is spread across multiple chapters.

Millie & Marv: When One Withdrawal Triggers Two Taxes

Millie and Marv spent four decades running a small arcade in a blue-collar town. Winters were long and brutal, with lake-effect storms routinely dropping a foot of snow. They survived by counting every nickel, dime, and quarter that moved through the machines, so discovering that the IRS takes a hidden second cut would have driven them crazy.

They are both seventy, receive $50,000 in combined Social Security, and need an additional $40,000 per year from savings to support their lifestyle. The variable is the account they use.

An IRA withdrawal counts as ordinary income, and it can trigger taxation on up to eighty-five percent of Social Security. A Roth withdrawal creates no taxable income, no Social Security taxation, and no federal income tax. At first glance, the Roth looks like an obvious answer. But that first glance leaves out the standard deduction, and that omission changes the calculation significantly. The table shows three versions of the same $40,000: the intuitive IRA calculation most people assume, the correct IRA calculation after deductions, and the Roth.

	IRA Only (intuitive calc)	IRA Only (correct calc)	Roth Only
Social Security Income	$50,000	$50,000	$50,000
IRA Withdrawal	$40,000	$40,000	$0
Roth Withdrawal	$0	$0	$40,000
Taxable SS (up to 85%)	$42,500	$42,500	$0
Adjusted Gross Income	$82,500	$82,500	$0
Standard Deduction	Not applied	**($35,500)**	N/A
Taxable Income	$82,500	$47,000	$0
Federal Income Tax	$9,404	$5,144	$0
After-Tax Spendable	**$80,596**	**$84,856**	**$90,000**

Note: Social Security taxation is simplified for illustration. Actual outcomes depend on combined income, deductions, and other income sources.

The difference between the IRA and the Roth is real but smaller than the intuitive math suggests. Sequencing matters because Social Security taxation can create higher effective marginal rates in specific income ranges.

Whether Roth conversions improve the result depends on the rate paid at conversion, the size and timing of future RMDs, Social Security, and other income sources. Millie and Marv's example shows the structure. The solution requires a coordinated plan.

For couples with significant traditional IRA balances, the most urgent coordination question is what happens to the survivor's tax picture when one spouse dies.

IRMAA: The Medicare Surcharge Most Retirees Don't See Coming

Most retirees pay the standard Medicare Part B and Part D premiums. When income exceeds certain levels, IRMAA surcharges are triggered. Unlike tax brackets, these are not gradual. They are fixed increases that apply to each taxpayer at each threshold. IRMAA is calculated on income from two years prior, before deductions. Neither the standard deduction nor itemized deductions reduce the income used to determine these surcharges. An IRA withdrawal, an asset sale, or a large RMD in one year can increase Medicare premiums by thousands of dollars two years later. This is why IRMAA belongs in the income plan, not as a surprise on the Medicare bill. Expressed as a percentage of income, the surcharges add one to three percentage points to the effective tax rate.

Current IRMAA Surcharges (Medicare Part B and Part D)

Single Filer	Married Filing Jointly	Part B Surcharge	Part D Surcharge	Combined Monthly	Annual Surcharge Per Person
≤ $109,000	≤ $218,000	$0	$0	$0	$0
$109,001 – $137,000	$218,001 – $274,000	$81.20	$14.50	$95.70	$1,148
$137,001 – $171,000	$274,001 – $342,000	$202.90	$36.60	$239.50	$2,874
$171,001 – $205,000	$342,001 – $410,000	$325.00	$58.70	$383.70	$4,604
$205,001 – $499,999	$410,001 – $749,999	$447.00	$77.30	$524.30	$6,292
≥ $500,000	≥ $750,000	$487.00	$91.00	$578.00	$6,936

Source: CMS 2026 Medicare Parts A & B Premiums and Deductibles. Surcharges shown are the amounts above the standard premium. For a married couple both on Medicare, the annual surcharge doubles. Based on income from two years prior (2024 tax return for 2026 premiums)

The widow's penalty applies here as well. A married couple with $200,000 in income pays no IRMAA surcharge. When one spouse dies, the survivor files as single with lower thresholds. The same $200,000 in income now triggers a $4,604 surcharge.

This is another cost that arrives automatically after the first death unless it is planned for in advance.

Both problems, the bracket compression and the IRMAA surcharge, are addressed together in Chapter 9, where Minnie and Jean's full remedy is modeled.

Ask Your Advisor Today – Social Security and Medicare
Survivor income: Beyond the tax bracket change, what happens to our Medicare premiums, Social Security taxation, and income control when one of us dies?
Conversion window: Have we identified the years when Roth conversions can be executed at the lowest rates and is there a written plan to use them?

Integration Check: Act II: Tax System and Retirement Assets

1. How will the widow's penalty affect the surviving spouse as our plan currently stands? When should we start a plan to address it?
2. How do our charitable giving options interact with Social Security taxation thresholds and IRMAA surcharge levels, and which vehicle produces the best combined result?
3. Given the current split across our tax-deferred, Roth, and taxable accounts, do we have enough flexibility to control income in retirement, or are we locked into a single bracket path?
4. If our RMDs begin today at their projected size, what do they trigger beyond the income tax bracket: Social Security taxation, IRMAA surcharges, or both?

ACT II CAPSTONE: Grant and Susan, The Benefits of Integrated Advice

Grant spent thirty-two years building brands for a luxury menswear company, the kind of work where presentation is everything and the gap between how something looks and what it actually is can be managed indefinitely, as long as nobody looks too closely.

Susan spent twenty years as a hand model. Her hands were insured, moisturized, and photographed for watch campaigns, jewelry catalogs, and the occasional luxury car brochure. She understood better than most that what appears in the frame and what exists outside it is rarely the same thing.

They retired at sixty-two, moved to Florida, and felt, for the first time in decades, that the hard work was done. The statement balances looked right.

Grant and Susan retired with $3,500,000 in a traditional IRA, $1,000,000 in a brokerage account, and no Roth. They spend $150,000 per year after tax. Grant's Social Security benefit at full retirement age is $42,000 annually. Susan's is $18,000. Florida has no state income tax, one genuine advantage they chose deliberately.

What follows is the same financial situation analyzed two ways. The assets are the same. The spending needs are the same. One version makes each decision independently. The other treats them as one coordinated system.

Scenario A: The Siloed Approach

Without a coordinating advisor, Grant and Susan make three decisions that each look reasonable on their own.

They both claim Social Security at sixty-two. The break-even analysis says waiting does not pay off until their late seventies, and they want to prioritize today. At sixty-two, Grant receives $29,400 and Susan receives $12,600, thirty percent lower than the full retirement age benefit. They fund their $150,000 spending from the IRA because they are still in a relatively low bracket early in retirement, and they skip Roth conversions. Why pay more taxes now when they do not have to?

The problem is what those decisions create together over time. The IRA keeps growing even as withdrawals are taken. By the time RMDs begin at seventy-three, the balance has risen to roughly $5.4 million. The first RMD is approximately $206,000. Combined with Social Security, they enter the RMD years already in the twenty-two percent bracket, and the mandatory withdrawals produce more after-tax income than they actually spend. The surplus flows into the brokerage. On the surface, the plan still looks fine.

The hidden cost is control. RMDs are taxed at whatever rate applies at the time. With no Roth, Grant and Susan have no flexibility to manage brackets, Medicare surcharges, or what happens to the surviving spouse's tax situation when one of them dies. The plan is functional, but rigid.

Scenario B: The Coordinated Plan

Now assume Grant and Susan work with an advisor who models retirement as one system rather than a set of separate decisions.

Decision One: Social Security is survivor planning. Grant delays to 70. His benefit starts at $52,080, permanently inflation-adjusted, and it becomes the survivor benefit that Susan steps up to if Grant dies first. Susan claims at sixty-two. As the lower earner, the early reduction matters less. If Grant dies first, she steps up to his benefit regardless of when she claimed. The integrated decision is the same: delay the higher earner, claim early for the lower one.

What the timing decision does not show is equally important: delaying Grant creates the most valuable tax window of their retirement, the years between sixty-two and sixty-seven when income is deliberately low and the conversion opportunity is wide open.

Decision Two: Convert during the window, spend from the brokerage. With only Susan's reduced Social Security showing up in the early years, taxable income is low by design. The advisor converts IRA dollars to Roth each year, filling the available bracket space. Living expenses come from the brokerage account, not the IRA. Brokerage withdrawals generate long-term capital gains only on the gain portion, taxed at 18.8 percent. An IRA withdrawal of the same amount is taxed entirely as ordinary income at twenty-two to twenty-four percent. Every IRA dollar that avoids a spending withdrawal is a dollar that moves to the Roth instead.

The conversion strategy runs in two phases. At age sixty-two, the conversion is done to the top of the twenty-four percent bracket. At age sixty-three, the conversion targets the MAGI of $342,000, the second IRMAA threshold. Since IRMAA surcharges at age 65 are based on income at age 63, the higher conversion at 62 doesn't affect IRMAA. The brokerage funds living expenses. The conversions continue to this threshold once RMDs begin. The continued conversion will help cap future IRMAA surcharges.

The brokerage runs out around age 67. After that, spending shortfalls are covered by the Roth. The IRA's only job from that point forward is to convert. By age 80, the IRA has been reduced from $3.5 million to roughly $874 thousand. The Roth holds over $8.5 million. The brokerage is empty.

Decision Three: IRMAA management is built into the conversion schedule. Medicare premiums carry income-based surcharges that most retirees discover only after they arrive. The coordinated plan treats IRMAA thresholds as hard constraints. During the aggressive conversion years, the household absorbs a modest surcharge because the conversion window is too valuable to leave unused. Once conversions slow, the IRMAA drops to zero and stays there. In the DIY plan, rising RMDs push IRMAA surcharges higher every year, an invisible cost that compounds alongside the visible ones.

What the Numbers Show

The coordinated plan never shows a higher statement balance. At age eighty, the DIY total is $10,378,000 against the advisor's $9,422,000. On every statement, the DIY plan looked like the better outcome.

Account Balances With Advisor

Age	IRA	Brok	Roth	Total	Heir Value
62	$3,329	$842	$416	$4,587	$2,923
65	$3,019	$370	$1,569	$4,958	$3,448
70	$2,392	$0	$3,442	$5,835	$4,639
73	$2,039	$0	$4,630	$6,669	$5,650
75	$1,760	$0	$5,567	$7,328	$6,448
80	$874	$0	$8,548	$9,422	$8,985

Account Balances DIY

Age	IRA	Brok	Roth	Total	Heir Value
62	$3,610	$1,060	$0	$4,670	$2,865
65	$3,994	$1,262	$0	$5,257	$3,260
70	$4,853	$1,689	$0	$6,543	$4,116
73	$5,444	$2,075	$0	$7,519	$4,797
75	$5,744	$2,494	$0	$8,239	$5,367
80	$6,378	$3,999	$0	$10,378	$7,188

All figures in thousands. Heir Value = IRA × 50% + Brokerage (step-up) + Roth (tax-free). "Phase" refers to the conversion strategy described above. Growth rates: IRA and Roth 7%, brokerage 6%. 2026 federal tax brackets, IRMAA thresholds, and RMD schedules.

But statement balances are not wealth. The DIY plan's $6.4 million IRA carries an embedded tax liability on every dollar. The advisor's $8.5 million Roth carries none. At age eighty, the roughly $956,000 account balance advantage for the DIY plan, is actually $1,797,000 less in after-tax wealth to their heirs.

The Survivor Test

Most retirement plans are built for the couple. The real test is whether the plan still works for whoever is left.

Assume one spouse dies at eighty. The survivor files as a single taxpayer from that point forward. Single brackets are narrower. The standard deduction is smaller. The same income that fit comfortably on a joint return now lands in a higher bracket, and the RMD does not adjust for any of it.

One Spouse Dies at 80, Survivor Files as Single

	With Advisor	DIY
IRA at 80 (thousands)	$874	$6,378
Roth at 80 (thousands)	$8,548	$0
Brokerage at 80 (thousands)	$0	$3,999
SS survivor benefit, annual	$52,080	$29,400
First RMD, age 81	$48,217	$328,786
Taxable income, age 81	$76,385	$336,026
Marginal bracket	22%	35%
Federal tax, year one	$11,719	$86,378
IRMAA surcharge, year one	$6,292	$6,358
Total tax + IRMAA, year one	$18,011	$92,736
Spending shortfall covered by	Roth (tax-free)	N/A, surplus
Heir value at 85 (thousands)	$12,101	$9,537
Heir value at 90 (thousands)	$16,510	$12,781
Heir value at 95 (thousands)	$22,711	$17,200

Assumes one spouse dies at 80 and the survivor files as a single taxpayer from age 81. IRMAA surcharge reflects Medicare Parts B and D for one person based on income from two years prior. Heir value = IRA × 50% + Brokerage (step-up) + Roth (tax-free).

In the DIY plan, the survivor inherits a $6.4 million IRA and a mandatory first RMD of $328,786. Combined with Social Security, the federal tax bill in the first full year of survivorship is $86,378. The survivor is in the thirty-five percent bracket, has no Roth to draw from, and cannot reduce taxable income. The plan that looked fine for the couple becomes punishing for the individual.

In the coordinated plan, the IRA is $874,000, and the Roth holds over $8.5 million. The first RMD is $48,217. The survivor remains in the twenty-two percent bracket. Federal tax is $11,719. The spending gap is covered by the Roth. The survivor spends the same amount, pays 86.4 percent less in federal tax, and holds an asset that continues to grow tax-free.

The IRMAA surcharges follow the same pattern. The coordinated plan's lower income drops the surcharge to near zero within three years. The DIY plan's RMDs keep it elevated for life.

Delaying Grant's Social Security created the low-income window that made nineteen years of Roth conversions possible at favorable rates. The Roth balance at 80, the tax savings, and the survivor protection are all direct results of treating these as one decision.

The Question Grant and Susan Actually Care About

Everything above assumes Grant and Susan spend $150,000 per year. The coordinated plan produces substantially more after-tax wealth. That raises the practical question: how much more can they spend while they are alive? They did not save for thirty years to live a frugal retirement.

The coordinated plan creates enough structural advantage that Grant and Susan can spend $193,000 per year and still leave their heirs more than what the DIY plan leaves at $150,000. This 28.6 percent more in annual spending, roughly $3,583 more per month, is funded by where the money sits and when it moves.

Advisor at $193,000 vs. DIY at $150,000

Age	Adv Total	Adv Heir	DIY Total	DIY Heir
80	$7,832	$7,395	$10,378	$7,188
85	$10,081	$9,623	$12,875	$9,537
90	$13,226	$12,788	$15,977	$12,781
95	$17,608	$17,243	$19,857	$17,200

Advisor scenario assumes $193,000 annual after-tax spending; DIY assumes $150,000. All figures in thousands. Heir Value = IRA × 50% + Brokerage (step-up) + Roth (tax-free). All other assumptions unchanged.

What Actually Changed

In every scenario the coordinated plan produced a better after-tax outcome. As a couple spending $150,000 per year, after-tax wealth was higher from the start. After the first death, the survivor paid 86 percent less in federal tax. At $193,000 per year, Grant and Susan spent 28.6 percent more, roughly $1.2 million over a lifetime, and still left heirs the same inheritance.

The total lifetime tax bill tells the story. The DIY plan paid $2,759,000 in federal taxes and IRMAA surcharges over 34 years. The coordinated plan paid $1,510,000. The difference, $1,249,000, came from the same income, the same assets, and the same spending. It was captured by architecture.

> **Rule Extracted:**
> A statement balance is not wealth. After-tax wealth is wealth.

Grant built his career on the difference between how things look and what they are actually worth. His retirement plan deserved the same scrutiny.

Ask Your Advisor Today – Capstone Grant and Susan

Statement balance vs. after-tax wealth: Show me my retirement projected two ways: decisions made independently versus coordinated as one system. What is the after-tax difference at ages eighty, eighty-five, and ninety?

Survivor test: If one of us dies at eighty, walk through the survivor's first full tax year: RMD, Social Security, filing status, IRMAA, and total tax burden, all in one number.

Spending capacity: Given our current plan structure, what is the maximum we can spend annually and still leave heirs at least as well off as the current plan projects?

From Tax Architecture to Income

Act III takes the next step: turning those static structures into a living income plan, deciding what to draw, from where, and when, so tax drag does not become forced income. The objective is to build the tax layer of the fortress so that after-tax income holds across decades, through both spouses' lifetimes, and into the next generation.

Modeling assumptions are summarized in the Appendix D1.

ACT III: Inflation, Income, and Timing

Act II mapped the tax system. Act III introduces the risk that makes every tax mistake more expensive over time: inflation. Inflation cannot be controlled. Neither can volatility or the tax code. What can be controlled is how exposed the plan is to all of them. A few years of elevated prices permanently reset what retirement costs. Avoidable taxes, unnecessary IRMAA surcharges, and bracket compression that could have been prevented all become more damaging when inflation is compounding on top of them. Lowering the structural cost of retirement is the most effective inflation defense available.

This act builds the income system that delivers it. It begins with inflation and the strategies that reduce its impact. It continues with tax timing, Roth conversions, and bracket management. It concludes with the tools that turn account balances into durable, after-tax income designed to hold when markets, prices, and longevity test the plan simultaneously.

Chapter 7: Inflation: The Risk You Cannot Reverse

> **Early Decision Rule:**
> Inflation is a cost floor that continually rises toward your fixed income ceiling. The squeeze does not reverse.

> **Reality Check:**
> Inflation does not reduce what you have. It increases the cost of what you need.

Volatility arrives suddenly and visibly. Markets crash, balances drop, and the pressure to act is immediate. But market declines can recover. Taxes build slowly and invisibly. A tax bomb grows for years inside a retirement account before RMDs and bracket compression reveal the cost. But future taxes can often be reduced with better planning. Inflation is the worst of both. It compounds steadily and cannot be restructured away like taxes. It spikes suddenly and forces bad decisions like volatility, but prices levels, once elevated, do not recover the way equity markets can. The damage from inflation is the annual increases compounding over time.

A plan that does not account for inflation gets squeezed between rising costs and a fixed income. That squeeze forces spending decisions that reshape retirement permanently.

Why Annual Rates Are Misleading

Annual inflation figures are misleading when read in isolation. They describe the rate of change over a single year, not the cumulative shift in the cost of living. Even a brief period of elevated prices permanently resets what retirement costs.

The 2021–2023 COVID inflation spike made this feel real. Headline CPI peaked at 9.1 percent year over year in June 2022, but the more important planning fact is that the price level moved substantially higher and stayed there. CPI-U rose from 262.045 in December 2020 to 326.031 in December 2025. That is a 24.4 percent increase over five years, or a compounded annual increase of approximately 4.5 percent. Even though the annual rate fell below 3 percent in both 2024 and 2025, the earlier price increases did not reverse. Future inflation is compounded on top of that higher base.

> **Reality Check:**
> Inflation is measured year over year. Its effect on purchasing power is cumulative.

What Can Actually Be Done

The conventional response to inflation is to invest more aggressively. Higher equity exposure, higher expected returns, more accumulated wealth to outpace rising prices. That logic works during accumulation. In retirement, it creates a different problem. A portfolio pushed toward higher returns also carries higher volatility, and volatility in retirement is the risk that can force behavioral decisions. Solving one problem creates another.

An integrated approach works both sides at once. Instead of relying solely on higher returns to outrun inflation, it also lowers the structural costs that inflate alongside prices. IRMAA surcharges, avoidable widow's penalty bracket compression, and forced taxable income from oversized RMDs are all expenses that grow more damaging as inflation compounds on top of them. Eliminating or reducing those costs is an inflation strategy, even though it looks like tax planning.

The strategies that follow in this act operate on both fronts. They reduce what retirement costs and increase what the income system can deliver. That combination is the most durable inflation defense available.

The First Design Choice: Essential vs. Discretionary Spending

The most practical first response to inflation is to separate spending into two categories from the beginning: essential and discretionary.

Essential spending:, housing, food, utilities, and basic healthcare, should be matched to reliable, inflation-aware income sources.

Discretionary spending is everything else. These lifestyle choices can be delayed, reduced, or re-sequenced without threatening the household's stability. Discretionary spending can tolerate more market dependence and more timing flexibility when costs rise unexpectedly.

When both categories draw from the same assets, retirees can end up making essential spending decisions based on market performance and driven by tax consequences rather than planning intent.

> **Reality Check:**
> Inflation does not affect every expense equally. A retirement income plan that treats all spending as interchangeable is just a withdrawal rate.

Social Security: The Core Inflation-Linked Mechanism

For most households, Social Security is the strongest inflation defense already built into the plan. It is lifetime income, government-backed, and adjusted annually for changes in the cost of living. Many retirees frame the claiming decision as a break-even exercise. That analysis is too narrow. The percentages are worth stating plainly. For a household with a full retirement age of sixty-seven, delaying from age sixty-two to full retirement age results in a 42.8 percent higher benefit. Further delaying from sixty-seven to seventy increases it another 24 percent. COLAs apply to every benefit regardless of when it is claimed. But a larger base produces a larger dollar increase with every adjustment. Essential expenses are paid in dollars, not percentages. The household that delays builds a permanently higher floor, and every future COLA widens the gap.

Grant and Susan: What Inflation Does to the Claiming Decision

The capstone held Social Security constant to isolate the tax architecture. This section adds inflation.

Social Security applies cost-of-living adjustments to the primary insurance amount every year, whether the benefit has been claimed or not. A larger starting benefit receives larger adjustments, and the gap between a small benefit and a large one widens every year for the rest of the recipient's life.

At sixty-two Grant had a claiming decision. He could receive $29,400 per year, inflation-adjusted going forward. Or he could delay to seventy. His base benefit at seventy before inflation adjustments is $52,080. But during the eight years of delay, the annual inflation adjustment is also growing the unclaimed benefit. Assuming 3.5 percent annual adjustments, the $29,400 he would have started receiving has grown to approximately $38,700 by age seventy. The benefit he deferred has grown to $68,579. The gap at seventy is nearly $30,000 per year, and it widens every year from there.

By eighty, the early benefit is approximately $54,600. The delayed benefit is approximately $96,700. The gap has grown from $30,000 to more than $42,000 per year. By ninety, the early benefit is approximately $77,000. The delayed benefit is approximately $136,500. The gap exceeds $59,000 per year.

If Grant predeceases Susan, she steps up to his benefit. A survivor who inherits a benefit of $96,700 at eighty lives a different retirement than a survivor who inherits $54,600. That difference compounds for the rest of her life.

Chapter 8 shows how Roth conversions, bracket management, and withdrawal timing reduce those structural costs. Chapter 9 shows how the income system is built to keep them low permanently.

TIPS, I-Bonds, and Inflation-Linked Assets

Social Security is not the only inflation-aware tool. Treasury Inflation-Protected Securities and Series I Savings Bonds can also play a role, when future spending obligations are known in advance.

Regular bonds promise fixed nominal dollars. TIPS protect the purchasing power of those dollars by adjusting principal with inflation. I-bonds offer a similar inflation adjustment with the added feature of tax deferral until redemption, though annual purchase limits and penalties for early redemption make them a supplemental tool rather than a core allocation.

Neither replaces the entire bond allocation. They are targeted instruments that fit naturally within the liquidity and stability capital layers. TIPS and I-bonds are most useful when the planning objective is preserving purchasing power in real terms rather than locking in a nominal yield. Capital earmarked for future spending should not grow at a rate that falls behind the prices it will eventually need to cover.

Tax-Free Accounts as Inflation-Response Tools

Inflation increases both spending and the tax cost of meeting that spending. When additional cash is drawn from taxable or tax-deferred accounts, the withdrawal can trigger collateral effects: more Social Security becomes taxable, IRMAA surcharges rise, and more income is exposed to higher effective rates.

Roth accounts, Health Savings Accounts used for qualified medical expenses, and properly structured cash-value life insurance function as reserve valves. A retiree who draws $10,000 from a Roth keeps the full amount. The same spending funded from a taxable or tax-deferred source requires a larger gross withdrawal to net the same dollars after tax and collateral effects. Fighting inflation means increasing income and keeping structural costs low.

The households that get squeezed in retirement are rarely the ones that saved too little. They are the ones whose income sources were never matched to their spending needs. Chapter 8 shows how to reduce the structural costs that make that mismatch more expensive every year.

Ask Your Advisor Today – Inflation and Income Design

Social Security timing: Have we evaluated the claiming decision as an inflation strategy, not just a break-even calculation, and what is the dollar difference in the inflation-adjusted floor at age 85?

Inflation Income: Which essential expenses are currently covered by inflation-aware income sources, and which are not?

Inflation Spending Reserves: If inflation forces an extra $10,000 to $20,000 annual spending, which account funds it and what are the tax consequences?

Income Plans: What does the income plan look like at 80 or 90 if prices continue rising faster than expected?

Chapter 8: Tax Timing: Creating More Income from the Same Assets

> **Early Decision Rule:**
> Tax problems in retirement are caused by forced income at high marginal rates without alternatives. The strategies in this chapter are implemented years before retirement. By the time income is forced, the window to create alternatives has closed.

Chapter 7 identified the structural costs that inflation makes more expensive every year: IRMAA surcharges, bracket compression, the widow's penalty, and oversized RMDs. This chapter shows how to reduce them. The primary tool is timing, controlling when income is recognized, at what rate, and from which account. A Roth conversion executed in a low-bracket year increases taxes now at a rate you choose. The payoff is permanent. Every converted dollar is removed from the pool of assets that will generate forced taxable income for decades, compounding through rising prices, into a surviving spouse's compressed brackets.

Required Minimum Distributions: The Tax Timing Problem

When retirement wealth is heavily concentrated in tax-deferred accounts, RMDs can force taxable income far beyond actual spending needs. That forced income can push households into higher marginal brackets, increase the taxable portion of Social Security benefits, and trigger Medicare premium surcharges through IRMAA.

RMDs are the moment tax deferral stops being optional. The only question that matters is whether that future schedule was priced correctly in advance.

> **Reality Check:**
> RMDs are a tax collection mechanism. Once they begin, the timing is set by the IRS, not by the retiree. The time to address RMD exposure is before it becomes mandatory.

Bryce's Mega Backdoor Roth Conversion Strategy

Bryce is 45, single, and earning $250,000 a year as the head test baker at a large food conglomerate. His signature creations, spinach quiche and pear pie, have become staples in the company's product line. He applies the same precision to retirement contributions that he applies to his recipes. That is how he found the provision most plan participants never notice.

He contributes the maximum $24,500 to his 401(k) as pre-tax contributions and receives a $12,000 employer match. His employer's plan also allows after-tax, non-Roth contributions up to the IRS aggregate limit of $72,000. That leaves $35,500 in after-tax space to reach the cap.

The plan also permits those after-tax contributions to be converted to Roth inside the plan. This is called an in-plan Roth conversion or a mega backdoor Roth. The principal has already been taxed, and converting immediately triggers little or no additional tax. What changes is the future tax character of the growth.

> **What This Means for You:**
> This strategy does not increase what Bryce saves. It changes how those savings are classified. The benefit does not appear now. It appears at age 73, when required minimum distributions begin and the split between taxable and tax-free assets determines the level of control he has.

Bryce converts $35,500 per year to Roth for 28 years alongside his traditional contributions. All investments grow at 7.5 percent annually. By age 73, his retirement assets are split between traditional and Roth accounts rather than concentrated entirely in the traditional 401(k). That split gives him control. His mandatory taxable RMD is roughly half of what it would have been without the strategy, his bracket drops from thirty-five to thirty-two percent, and his federal tax bill falls by $42,919.

	Without Mega Backdoor	With Mega Backdoor	Difference
Traditional 401(k)	$6,786,379	$3,440,317	$3,346,062 less
Roth (in-plan conversion)	$0	$3,346,062	$3,346,062 more
Other income	$100,000	$100,000	
RMD at 73	**$256,090**	**$129,823**	**$126,267 less**
Total taxable income	$356,090	$229,823	
Marginal bracket	**35%**	**32%**	**−1 bracket**
Federal tax	$87,766	$44,847	$42,919 less
Effective tax rate	**24.65%**	**19.52%**	**5.13 pts less**
After-tax income	$268,324	$184,976	
Roth withdrawal needed	N/A	$83,348	
Total spendable	**$268,324**	**$268,324**	**Equal**

Assumptions: $35,500 per year to Roth and $36,500 per year to traditional for 28 years at 7.5% growth (ages 45–73). RMD divisor: 26.5 per IRS Uniform Lifetime Table. 2026 single-filer brackets, $16,100 standard deduction, and $100,000 of other income assumed. Spendable income equals after-tax income plus any tax-free Roth withdrawal.

The result is $42,919 less in federal tax, with the same spendable income. His smaller taxable RMD makes the Roth a relief valve. He supplements his income from that account. His effective tax rate drops by five percentage points, from 24.65 to 19.52 percent, because less of his income is mandated by RMDs. The same assets produce more after-tax purchasing power because less is claimed by the IRS each year. That is the advantage. Not a higher return. More control over what is kept.

> **Rule Extracted:**
> Bracket management is the advantage. Contribution reclassification is the tool. The window is during the working years.

Bryce's strategy works because he is reclassifying contributions before they grow. The next two case studies test the conversion decision itself. Dora shows what happens when the rate is wrong. Jessie shows what happens when it is right, and what it means for the people who inherit what is left.

Dora's Roth Conversion: When "Pay Now" Isn't Automatically Better

Roth conversions are often framed as a simple trade: pay tax now to avoid tax later. Dora's situation shows why that framing is incomplete.

Dora is fifty-three, single, and at the top of her game. As the leading producer at The Good Party Planners, the city's premier event-planning firm, she has spent her career engineering flawless events for other people. At every marquee event, she was easy to spot, usually in her signature polka dots. She earns $275,000 a year and is considering converting $100,000 from her traditional IRA to a Roth while sitting in a thirty-five percent marginal bracket.

The idea sounded sensible. Pay tax now, avoid tax later, and move more money into the tax-free bucket. Dora was used to coordinating every detail carefully. But this decision had not been fully modeled. To pay the conversion tax, she would have to sell appreciated taxable assets, turning a future tax question into an immediate tax bill and reducing the capital left to compound. The issue was whether paying thirty-five percent now to avoid a lower rate later made economic sense.

The Immediate Cost

Converting $100,000 creates a $35,000 federal tax bill. To pay it, she sells $40,000 of taxable securities, with the extra covering capital gains tax on the sale. The real cost is the capital removed from the portfolio that no longer compounds.

The Growth Comparison

Assume 7.5 percent annual growth over 20 years. The IRA grows to $424,785 whether it stays traditional or becomes Roth. The outcome hinges on the $40,000 she sold to pay the conversion tax. That capital would have grown to approximately $169,914.

Under these assumptions, the conversion reduces Dora's after-tax value at age seventy-two by $38,541 once forgone after tax growth is included. Converting at thirty-five percent to avoid a projected twenty-four percent retirement bracket is tax acceleration, not tax optimization. It is paying $35 today to avoid $24 later.

Dora: No Conversion vs. Convert to Roth

	No Conversion	Convert to Roth
Tax Paid Now	$0	$35,000
Securities Sold to Pay Tax	$0	$40,000
IRA Growth (20 yrs @ 7.5%)	$424,785	$424,785
Opportunity Cost	$0	$140,489
Taxes at Withdrawal (24%)	$101,948	$0
NET SPENDABLE	**$322,837**	**$284,296**

Opportunity cost reflects $40,000 in securities sold to fund the conversion tax, grown at 7.5% for 20 years, shown after capital gains tax on the accumulated gain.

When a Conversion Does Make Sense

Dora's case is specific: high current bracket and fund IRA conversion by selling appreciated assets. The math does not work for her right now.

The same analysis looks very different for someone in a lower tax bracket between retirement and forced RMDs. Converting at twenty-two percent to avoid a projected thirty-two percent bracket and paying the tax from cash rather than by selling appreciated securities will produce a more favorable outcome.

> **Decision Rule:**
> A Roth conversion is tax optimization when the rate paid today is lower than the rate avoided later, and the tax can be funded without selling assets needed for compounding. Otherwise, it is prepayment at a premium.

Jessie's case is exactly the opposite scenario, and it adds one more dimension Dora's story does not: what happens to the money after the owner dies.

Jessie: The Window Is Wider Than It Looks

Jessie retired at sixty-two with a tidy coincidence: her salary had been $100,000, her annual spending was $100,000, and her retirement income, pension plus Social Security, was also $100,000. Nothing changed at the lifestyle level. Everything changed at the tax level.

With spending fully covered, she had no reason to touch her $2,000,000 traditional 401(k). Left alone, growing at seven percent annually, it would reach $4.2 million by age seventy-two and force taxable distributions for the rest of her life. Her daughter Syd would inherit the remainder. The SECURE Act requires inherited IRAs to be distributed within ten years. Every dollar withdrawn from the inherited IRA would stack on top of Syd's existing income, pushing her into the thirty-seven percent bracket.

A large traditional IRA is the owner's tax problem and becomes the heir's tax problem the day it is inherited.

Jessie had one goal: maximize what Syd receives after tax. The Roth conversion window was the tool.

The Window Is Not Where You Think It Is

Most investors assume the Roth conversion window opens at retirement, when income falls and bracket room appears. That assumption should be scrutinized.

The conversion decision is triggered by tax rate spread, not retirement status. If the tax rate you pay today is lower than the tax rate RMDs impose later, then conversion should be considered.

Jessie's $100,000 salary placed her taxable income at $83,900, inside the twenty-two percent bracket, with $117,875 of room to the top of the twenty-four percent bracket. The blended conversion rate during her working years was 23.6 percent, the same rate available to her in retirement.

The optimal scenario in the table starts at age fifty-four. At seven percent annual growth, the $2,000,000 IRA at age sixty-two discounts back to $1,164,018 at age fifty-four. Converting to the top of the twenty-four percent bracket through working years and into retirement empties the traditional IRA by age seventy, before RMDs begin. The Roth then compounds untouched for fifteen years. Syd receives $7.75 million after tax.

Starting at sixty-two, which is the window Jessie actually used, still produces $7.13 million for Syd at the same 23.6 percent blended rate. She used the window she could see, and it still worked. The lesson is not that Jessie "should have" started earlier. It is that the window is often wider than it appears.

The optimal conversion starts as early as the rate spread justifies. Converting too early, at an unnecessarily high rate, reduces compounding. Waiting too long can turn deferral into forced income or transfer the tax problem to an heir at a higher rate.

What the Table Shows

Jessie For Syd	No Conversion	Start at 62	Optimal (Age 54)
Setup			
IRA at age 62	$2,000,000	$2,000,000	$2,000,000 [1]
Conversion start age	—	62	54
Conversion years	0	11 (ages 62–72)	19 (ages 54–72)
IRA reaches zero	Never	Never	Age 70
Total conversion tax paid	$0	$348,955	$478,140
Effective conversion rate	—	23.6%	23.6%
Age 72: End of Conversion Window			
IRA	$4,209,704	$2,254,511	$0
Roth	$0	$1,494,723	$3,216,415
Total account balances at 72	**$4,209,704**	**$3,749,233**	**$3,216,415**
Ages 73–85: RMD Years			
Total RMD taken	$3,300,962	$1,560,366	$0 [2]
Total federal tax paid	$1,104,032	$597,859	$0 [2]
Effective tax rate (73–85)	24.0%	20.0%	—
Age 85: Balances at Death			
IRA	$5,316,535	$2,709,974	$0
Roth	$0	$3,781,601	$7,751,062
Brokerage (after-tax RMDs reinvested)	$3,217,638	$1,644,176	$0
Post-Tax Value at Death: What Syd Receives			
IRA tax @37%	$1,967,118	$1,002,690	$0
IRA post-tax	$3,349,417	$1,707,284	$0

Jessie For Syd	No Conversion	Start at 62	Optimal (Age 54)
Roth	$0	$3,781,601	$7,751,062
Step-Up Brokerage	$3,217,638	$1,644,176	$0
TOTAL POST-TAX WEALTH TO SYD	**$6,567,055**	**$7,133,061**	**$7,751,062**
Advantage over no conversion	—	**+$566,006**	**+$1,184,007**

[1] Optimal scenario uses the equivalent value at age 54 that compounds to $2,000,000 by age 62 at 7%.
[2] IRA reaches zero at age 70. No RMDs required ages 73–85.
Assumptions: $2,000,000 traditional 401(k) at age 62. Income of $100,000 throughout: salary ages 54–61, Social Security plus pension ages 62–85. Spending fully covered in all scenarios. 7% annual growth in all accounts. 2026 single-filer brackets. Conversion tax is paid from converted amount. After-tax RMD net deposited to taxable brokerage annually. Post-tax value assumes IRA taxed at 37%, brokerage stepped up at death, and Roth fully after-tax. No state tax.

Dora shows that "convert now" is not automatically right. Jessie shows the opposite case: sometimes the window exists even while you are still working. In the optimal scenario, Jessie has no RMDs at all, which also means no IRMAA surcharges triggered by forced income she does not need.

Tax Deferral Is Not Tax Efficiency

Jessie shows what it costs when a large traditional IRA is left to compound unchecked, not in returns, but in the rate the IRS eventually charges on every forced dollar. The conversion window is defined by rate spread, not retirement status. Her working-year bracket was identical to her retirement bracket. The window was already open at fifty-four. Every unconverted dollar cost Syd 37 cents on a mandatory ten-year distribution schedule.

For married couples, the arithmetic is even more compelling. The widow's penalty compresses brackets at the first death, RMDs continue, and IRMAA surcharges can increase sharply on the same income. A smaller IRA and a larger Roth change that trajectory for both the owner and the heir. Lower forced income, more control over brackets, and more after-tax dollars available to spend during retirement. More left to transfer after it. This is why conversions have to be modeled, not assumed. The answer depends on brackets, spending needs, future RMDs, and the heir's likely tax rate.

Chapter 9 takes the next step, from bracket management into the broader problem of engineering retirement income that holds regardless of what markets, taxes, or longevity demand from it.

Ask Your Advisor Today – Tax Timing and Bracket Management

Income forecast: Where does my retirement income come from by account type and what does forced income from RMDs do to my brackets and Medicare premiums?

Conversion window: For each case study in this chapter, Bryce, Dora, and Jessie, which scenario most closely matches my situation, and what does the math look like with my actual numbers?

Chapter 9: Constructing Income: Structure and Certainty

Chapter 7 showed that inflation raises the cost of retirement permanently. Chapter 8 showed how tax timing and bracket management reduce the structural costs that inflation compounds. This chapter builds the income system itself. Two case studies show the two ways it is done: creating more income from the same assets through tax architecture and securing income that cannot be outlived through contractual structure.

> **Early Decision Rule:**
> A portfolio does not become a paycheck on its own. The job is to build a cash-flow system that holds when markets, prices, and longevity test it simultaneously.

Minnie and Jean: What the Remedy Looks Like

Chapter 4 showed what the widow's penalty costs when it arrives without preparation: a compressed tax bracket increased total taxes even as total income fell. That problem can be addressed in advance. Here we revisit Minnie and Jean eleven years before their first RMD is due and implement a plan designed to produce the same after-tax lifestyle with a much better long-term outcome.

At age sixty-two, they have the same income profile used earlier: an $80,000 pension, $40,000 each in Social Security, and a $1,885,976 traditional IRA, the exact balance that grows at seven percent annually to produce a $140,000 RMD at age seventy-three.

Two decisions define the plan.

1. Delay Social Security to age seventy.
This is a claiming strategy and a conversion strategy.

One spouse claims Social Security at sixty-two, producing $40,000 per year to help support living expenses. The other delays to age seventy, locking in a $71,000 benefit instead of $40,000. During the eight-year window from age sixty-two through sixty-nine, the lower combined income creates room to convert IRA dollars at the top of the twenty-four percent married-filing-jointly bracket. That room narrows once both Social Security checks begin.

When one spouse dies, the $40,000 benefit disappears. The $71,000 delayed benefit is the income floor the survivor will live on for the rest of life.

2. Convert aggressively during pre-70 window.
Each year from ages sixty-two through sixty-nine, the couple converts to the top of the twenty-four percent bracket, "tax to the max." The conversions are taxed at a blended rate of 22.6 percent. Those converted dollars do triple duty: they cover the tax bill, help fund the spending gap created by delaying one Social Security benefit, and build the Roth balance.

By the end of age sixty-nine:

- Traditional IRA: $0
- Roth IRA: $2,002,822

Total conversion tax paid: $570,477 at a blended rate of 22.6 percent. This is a deliberate decision to pay tax now. The alternative is to remain exposed to the higher effective rates that forced RMDs will impose later.

At age seventy, the delayed $71,000 Social Security benefit begins. After federal tax, combined income exceeds their lifestyle need by $10,303 per year. That surplus flows into a taxable brokerage account. By age seventy-two, just before the first

RMD year would have begun, the IRA is $0, the Roth holds $2,453,543, and the brokerage account holds $33,123.

The goal was to reduce the impact of the widow's penalty. Because the plan leaves no RMD exposure, the widow's penalty largely disappears. At age 73, with proper planning, the survivor files as single on $151,000 of income, $80,000 of pension and $71,000 from the delayed survivor benefit. She pays $22,418 in federal tax and remains in the twenty-four percent marginal bracket. Her lifestyle, of $128,582 after tax, is fully funded by pension and Social Security alone. The Roth remains untouched.

The survivor without planning faces a very different result. The income includes the same pension, but a smaller survivor benefit, $40,000 instead of $71,000. To reach the same after-tax spending level, part of the $140,000 annual RMD must be used. That RMD does three things at once: it satisfies a government mandate, funds the tax created by that mandate, and partially supports her lifestyle.

The IRMAA surcharge adds another layer to the widow's penalty. At age seventy-three, the survivor with the plan has $151,000 in income pays $2,874 in annual surcharges. The survivor without the plan has $260,000 in income and pays $6,292. That is a $3,418 annual difference on top of the higher tax bill she is already paying. RMDs grow over time, which means the surcharge can increase further if the next threshold is crossed. Even as a married couple, the gap exists: without a plan they pay $2,874 per person while with a plan they pay $1,148 per person. Both paths carry a widow's penalty. A comprehensive retirement plan reduces the penalty. The IRMAA was not included in the aggregate analysis detailed on the next pages.

At Age 73: The Fork in the Road

Scenario	IRA Balance	Roth Balance	Federal Tax	After-Tax Lifestyle
No Plan Survivor	$3,710,000	$0	$52,584	$128,582 (plus excess RMD to brokerage)
Survivor with Plan	$0	$2,453,543	$22,418	$128,582 (no RMD, no Roth draw)

Simplified illustration using 2026 federal brackets and standard deduction. Assumptions are described in Appendix D3.

Both survivors spend the same $128,582 after tax. The planned survivor needs no RMD, no Roth withdrawal, and pays less than half the tax.

The Compounding Advantage (Ages 75–90)

For the rest of her life, the survivor spends the same lifestyle amount each year. What changes is how much she pays in tax and what is left after the IRS takes its share.

Scenario	IRA Balance	Roth Balance	Broker-age	Total-Tax (No Heir)	Heir Post Tax Value*
Age 75 No Plan	$4.03M		$0.27M	$167,210	$2.81M
Age 75 with Plan		$3.01M	$0.04M	$67,254	$3.05M
Age 80 No Plan	$4.48M		$1.03M	$520,185	$3.85M
Age 80 with Plan		$4.22M	$0.06M	$179,344	$4.27M
Age 85 No Plan	$4.69M		$2.35M	$991,835	$5.30M
Age 85 with Plan		$5.91M	$0.08M	$291,434	$5.99M

Scenario	IRA Balance	Roth Balance	Broker-age	Total-Tax (No Heir)	Heir Post Tax Value*
Age 90 No Plan	$4.48M		$4.50M	$1,604,358	$7.32M
Age 90 with Plan		$8.29M	$0.11M	$403,524	$8.40M

Simplified illustration. Assumptions are described in Appendix D3. All growth rates, brackets, and spending held constant. IRMAA surcharges are referenced in the text but not reflected in these figures. Results are directional, not predictive."
*Heir Post-Tax Value: IRA taxed at 37%; brokerage receives step-up in basis; Roth passes tax-free.

Over a seventeen-year survivor period, the unplanned path pays tax twice: first through lifetime income tax, and then through the tax heirs owe when they empty the inherited IRA. The cumulative-tax column isolates lifetime income tax. The heir post-tax column layers in the heirs' IRA tax by reducing the remaining IRA by 37 percent and crediting brokerage and Roth at full value.

Tax Summary: from age seventy-three through age ninety:

- **Unplanned cumulative tax paid:** $1,604,358
- **Planned cumulative tax paid:** $403,524
- **Tax savings:** $1,200,834
- **Planned heir advantage at age 90:** $1,083,697

The drag was real. It was also optional.

Minnie and Jean's remedy created more income from the same assets by changing the tax architecture. The next case study addresses a different problem: what happens when the income has to last longer than the assets can guarantee and every additional year increases the inflation exposure.

Rule Extracted:
The conversion window is finite. The tax savings compound permanently. Eight years of deliberate action at 22.6 cents on the dollar eliminated a survivor tax problem that would have cost four times as much left unaddressed.

Guaranteed Income: What Annuities Do

Annuities address specific risks: longevity, sequence, and behavioral pressure. Payouts vary by age, structure, and guarantees. Some provide immediate lifetime income. Others defer the start date, which increases the contractual payout rate. For longer planning horizons, income riders attached to insurance contracts can serve a similar purpose.

Annuities are not appropriate for every household. They trade liquidity for guarantees, and that trade only makes sense when the gap between guaranteed income and essential spending justifies the cost.

Herschel's Retirement Income Analysis: Certainty, Longevity, and the Cost of Control

Herschel ran a wine shop for thirty years on the second floor of a building, which he thought was the funniest thing in the world. "Come on upstairs to the cellar," he told every customer. Most of them laughed. All of them came back.

He knew better than most that the best things take time. A good Bordeaux does not apologize for aging well. Neither did Herschel. At seventy, with $2,000,000 saved and a need to produce $143,200 in annual income for life, Herschel compares two strategies. Both are funded from his traditional IRA, so the tax treatment is the same.

The Two Options

The first is an annuity that makes annual payments of $143,200 for the rest of his life, with a guarantee that at least twenty years will be paid, even if Herschel passes away before then. The payout rate is 7.16 percent, and the income is contractual, permanent, and does not depend on markets, interest rates, or how long Herschel lives.

The second is a bond portfolio yielding 4.25 percent annually. At that yield, $2,000,000 produces $85,000 in interest per year. To reach $143,200 in spending, Herschel must liquidate approximately $58,200 of principal in year one, a number that grows each year as the portfolio shrinks and interest income declines. The bond portfolio retains full liquidity and passes any remaining balance to his heirs. It also retains full longevity risk, if Herschel lives long enough, the money runs out.

Component	20-Yr Certain Annuity	Treasury 4.25%
Initial Investment	$2,000,000	$2,000,000
Annual Income	$143,200	$143,200
Interest (Year 1)	N/A	$85,000
Principal (Year 1)	$0	$58,200
Portfolio Depletes	Never	~Age 90
Beneficiary	Remaining payments	Balance
LONGEVITY RISK	**Eliminated**	**Retained by Herschel**

Table Footnote: Illustrative only. Payout rate is a contractual income factor, not an investment return. Guarantees depend on the insurer's claims-paying ability; annuitization reduces liquidity and may be difficult to reverse.

The annuity resolves longevity risk by design. The bond portfolio does not. If Herschel dies early, the twenty-year guarantee ensures payments continue to his heirs, though structured as annual payments rather than a lump sum. The structural difference is what happens if he does not die early.

The bond portfolio is steadily spending itself down, and that process does not stop.

Why After-Tax Annuity Income is Different
In this illustration, Herschel purchases the annuity with after-tax dollars. Each payment is split by the exclusion ratio between return of principal, which is tax-free, and earnings, which are taxable. Until the original $2,000,000 has been fully recovered, $100,000 per year is non-taxable return of principal and the remaining $43,200 is taxable ordinary income.

Herschel also receives $50,000 per year in Social Security and $50,000 per year from a pension from his first career. For simplicity, eighty-five percent of Social Security is assumed taxable, Herschel takes the standard deduction including the age adjustment, and there is no state income tax.

The bond portfolio is engineered to match the annuity's after-tax cash flow each year, so the comparison is honest. Early on, a larger share of the withdrawal comes from interest. As the bond portfolio shrinks, interest declines and more spending must come from principal. The principal is finite.

Herschel: Annuity vs. Bond Portfolio

		Annuity		Bond Portfolio		
Yr	Age	Non-Tax	Taxable	Non-Tax	Taxable	Balance
1	71	$100k	$43k	$68k	$85k	$1,932k
5	75	$100k	$43k	$77k	$73k	$1,636k
10	80	$100k	$43k	$91k	$55k	$1,209k
15	85	$100k	$43k	$106k	$35k	$709k
18	88	$100k	$43k	$117k	$21k	$368k
19	89	$100k	$43k	$121k	$16k	$247k
20	90	$100k	$43k	$125k	$11k	$122k
21	91	**$0**	**$143k**	**$103k**	**$5k**	**$19k**
22	92	**$0**	**$143k**	**$19k**	**$1k**	**Zero**

Simplified illustration. Assumes stated tax treatment, constant yields/returns, and simplified taxation. Actual results depend on rates, inflation, tax law, and individual circumstances. Not a guarantee. All dollars rounded to nearest thousand.

In years one through twenty, the annuity's non-taxable component keeps taxable income lower than the bond portfolio. In year twenty-one, the exclusion ratio ends and the full $143,200 becomes taxable. That shift is predictable and manageable. In year twenty-two, the bond portfolio runs out. Herschel is ninety-two. The annuity is still paying.

> **Rule Extracted:**
> Longevity risk is managed by structuring income that does not depend on still having money at ninety-two. Having enough at seventy solves nothing if the principal is gone before you are.

The higher annuity payout is not a magic yield. It reflects three components working together: the insurer's underlying investment return, return of principal embedded in each payment, and mortality credits created when longevity risk is pooled across many policyholders. Those three components allow a lifetime annuity to pay more current income than a bond portfolio with the same stated principal. The trade-off is reduced liquidity in exchange for longevity transfer and contractual income.

Rethinking the Four Percent Rule

The four percent rule is widely cited because it is simple: withdraw four percent annually from a portfolio to fund retirement spending. It is a withdrawal convention, not an income strategy. The entire portfolio must stay invested and exposed to market volatility to continue producing income. Sequence risk, longevity risk, behavioral pressure, and timing risk all remain with the retiree. The income may look sustainable on a spreadsheet. The lived experience can diverge sharply from the projection.

Lifetime income structures solve a different problem. They do not promise better returns. They remove sequence risk from the income itself and transfer longevity risk away from the retiree. Stability is what they deliver.

Accessing Capital Without Creating a Tax Event

Sometimes the income system needs liquidity that does not come from a withdrawal. Home equity and portfolio lending can both serve that role.

A reverse mortgage allows access to home equity with no required payments while the home remains a primary residence. The loan balance grows and is repaid at sale, move-out, or death. The trade-offs are cost and reduced flexibility.

A home-equity investment agreement involves no monthly payments and no interest but requires sharing future appreciation and depreciation. It converts equity into planning capital rather than debt, at the cost of surrendering part of the home's future upside.

A securities-based line of credit allows borrowing against a portfolio without selling assets. No sale means no capital gain, no bracket impact, and no IRMAA consequence. The trade-off is interest cost and the risk of a margin call if the portfolio declines.

Home equity and portfolio lending are liquidity tools. They prevent forced sales and taxable events.

Withdrawal Sequencing: Which Account First

The conventional sequence, taxable first, then tax-deferred, and Roth last, is a starting point, not a rule. In low-income years, drawing from tax-deferred accounts or converting to Roth can reduce future RMD pressure. In high-income years, Roth withdrawals can limit bracket exposure and minimize IRMAA surcharges.

The advantage is the flexibility to adjust the sequence year by year based on income, taxes, and spending needs. A plan that works perfectly under one set of assumptions but fails badly under another is a bet, not a plan. Multiple income sources, multiple tax treatments, and clear sequencing rules keep spending decisions from depending on any single market outcome, tax result, or lifespan assumption.

Ask Your Advisor Today – Constructing Income: Structure and Certainty

Longevity risk: What specific structure in my plan ensures income continues if I live past ninety, and what happens if it doesn't?

Annuity tax treatment: If an annuity makes sense, should it be funded with pre-tax or after-tax dollars, and how does that change the after-tax income?

Withdrawal sequencing: What is the assumed rule for which account funds spending first, and under what conditions does that order change?

Integration Check: Act III: Inflation, Income, and Timing

1. Have we modeled the Roth conversion window with a bracket target for each year and approximated when we should start?
2. Has the withdrawal sequencing rule been stress-tested against a scenario where one spouse dies early, inflation runs high, or markets decline sharply in the first five years?
3. Which guaranteed income sources cover essential expenses, and what is the gap if one of them stops?

ACT III CAPSTONE: Big Red, The Cost of Siloed Advice

Big Red spent thirty years as a world-renowned bird migration specialist. She tracked Ruby-crowned Kinglets from the Yucatán to the Canadian boreal forest, documented Blue Jay population corridors across the Atlantic flyway, and published research that other scientists cited for decades. She understood better than almost anyone that patterns have consequences. A species following the wrong route, or timing its migration badly, pays a price that compounds over thousands of miles.

She never applied that thinking to her own financial plan.

Big Red retired at sixty-two with a pension of $50,000 a year, $1,750,000 in a traditional IRA, and Social Security of $30,000 available immediately or $53,143 if she waited until seventy. She spent $80,000 a year. Her brother Dash, an MP in the Army, was her beneficiary.

The plan felt solid. The pension and Social Security covered her lifestyle. The IRA would keep growing, an untouched legacy for Dash one day. She had no long-term care coverage and no explicit plan for it. She did not think she needed one.

In retirement, Big Red mostly stayed home with Honeydew, her parakeet. The migrations she had spent her life documenting, the birds she had followed across hemispheres, the flyways she had mapped through decades of fieldwork, were still out there. She just never felt quite flush enough to follow them.

That was the plan working exactly as it had been built: carefully, rigidly, and without any awareness of the cost.

The Decisions, One at a Time

Decision One: Claiming Social Security at Sixty-Two
Big Red ran the break-even analysis. At $30,000 now versus $53,143 at seventy, the break-even age was eighty. She knew RMDs would be large enough to cover the difference from claiming early and preferred more cash now.

Her reasoning was not wrong, but she did not quantify the true cost.

Her $50,000 pension already ensured that up to eighty-five percent of her Social Security would be taxable regardless of when she claimed. More importantly, claiming early filled the low-income window between sixty-two and seventy, the years before RMDs began, with taxable income that crowded out Roth conversions. Every dollar of Social Security she activated early was a dollar of IRA conversion capacity she gave up at the lowest bracket rates she was likely to see again.

She optimized Social Security in isolation. She should have coordinated Social Security with IRA timing.

Decision Two: Leaving the IRA Untouched
From sixty-two to seventy-two, Big Red lived on her pension and Social Security. She did not touch the IRA, viewing it as a legacy for Dash. At seven percent annual growth, $1,750,000 trends toward $3.6 to $3.7 million by age seventy-two.

Decision Three: Ignoring Future RMDs
At seventy-three, her first required minimum distribution arrived. The IRA she had never touched was now about $3.8 million. Her required distribution was roughly $139,000, whether she needed the money or not.

Combined with her pension and Social Security, gross income jumped to roughly $219,000 and continued rising as the IRA grew and the RMD percentage increased. Her federal marginal bracket moved to thirty-two percent. IRMAA surcharges began layering onto her Medicare premiums. She still thought of herself as someone who lived on $80,000. The tax code did not care.

She increased spending modestly and saved the rest in a taxable brokerage account. The investments were not the problem. The problem was where the dollars accumulated, and at whose marginal rate they would eventually be taxed.

Decision Four: The Long-Term Care Blind Spot

At eighty-seven, her health declined. Long-term care costs ran about $150,000 a year above normal living expenses. She funded care from the taxable brokerage account because capital gains rates seemed more efficient than additional IRA withdrawals.

The logic was locally correct and structurally wrong. The brokerage account was heading toward a step-up in basis at death, effectively eliminating its embedded gains for Dash. The IRA carried no such treatment. Every dollar her brother received from the IRA would be taxed as ordinary income at a combined rate approaching forty-five percent. Preserving the IRA and depleting the brokerage shifted taxes from zero percent to Dash's full marginal rate.

The End Result

At age ninety, Big Red's estate held about $4.91 million in nominal assets: a $4.45 million traditional IRA and a $461,000 taxable brokerage account.

The brokerage passed largely with step-up treatment. The IRA had to be fully distributed within ten years. At Dash's combined marginal rate of roughly 45 percent, the federal and state income tax bill on that IRA exceeded $2 million.

Dash received about $2.91 million after tax, roughly 65 cents of every dollar Big Red had saved.

Structure, not recklessness, determined that outcome.

What the Integrated Plan Would Have Done

The integrated alternative reversed two decisions, added one tool, and changed the funding logic. Everything else stayed the same.

Step One: Delay Social Security to Build the Inflation-Protected Floor
Instead of claiming at sixty-two, Big Red delays to seventy. The benefit rises from $30,000 to $53,143 a year, permanently inflation adjusted. Every future cost-of-living adjustment compounds on the larger base.

For a single retiree, there is no spouse to step up. The benefit Big Red claims is the benefit she lives on. Delaying builds the strongest possible foundation for essential spending in every year that follows.

Step Two: Open the Roth Conversion Window
The delay creates something equally valuable. The years between sixty-two and seventy become a Roth conversion window. Without Social Security filling the lower brackets, Big Red converts portions of the traditional IRA annually, targeting the top of the twenty-four percent bracket.

By the time RMDs begin, the IRA balance is much smaller. The mandatory income that arrives at seventy-three is a fraction of what it would have been. IRMAA surcharges are reduced or eliminated. Her effective tax rate across ages sixty-two through ninety drops from 27.4 percent to 22.6 percent, a 4.8-point reduction. The tax savings are not spent. They compound inside the Roth and flow directly to Dash.

That was the number that changed Big Red's retirement. With less forced income and more flexibility, the coordinated plan showed her she could spend more, not recklessly, but deliberately. The Ruby-crowned Kinglets were still migrating.

The Blue Jays were still moving through the Atlantic flyway. For the first time, the plan showed her she could follow them.

Honeydew stayed home. Big Red did not have to.

Step Three: Transfer the Long-Term Care Risk
During the early retirement years, Big Red purchased long-term care coverage with level premiums of about $12,710 annually for ten years, securing roughly $600,000 of future benefits for a total premium outlay of $127,100. That is a 4.7-to-1 ratio of benefits to premiums. When care costs arrive at eighty-seven, insurance pays first.

Without the policy, every dollar of care is funded from Big Red's own accounts at whatever tax rate applies. With the policy, the most expensive years of her life are covered by dedicated capital that was put in place when the cost was lowest and the options were widest.

Step Four: Fund Care from the Right Account
In the no-action path, Big Red funded care from the brokerage because capital gains rates seemed more efficient than IRA withdrawals. That logic was backwards. The brokerage was headed toward a step-up in basis at death. Its embedded gains would have disappeared entirely for Dash. The IRA carried no such treatment. Every dollar Dash inherited from the IRA would be taxed at roughly forty-five percent. The real comparison was never thirty-five percent now versus fifteen percent now. It was thirty-five percent now versus forty-five percent later, while the brokerage was moving toward zero percent either way.

In the integrated plan, this problem does not arise. The IRA is depleted before care begins, and insurance covers the care costs. The Roth and any remaining brokerage assets transfer to Dash intact.

Side by Side

	No-Action Path	Integrated Path
IRA Balance at 90	$4,452,883	$0
Roth Balance at 90	$0	$3,883,135
Brokerage Balance	$460,577	$0
Heir Value (after tax)	**$2,909,663**	**$3,883,135**
After-Tax Difference		**+$973,472 (33%)**

	No-Action Path	Integrated Path
Total Lifetime Taxes Paid	$1,842,817	$1,288,722
Tax Savings		**$554,095**
Total Lifetime After-Tax Income	$4,871,092	$4,412,040
Effective Tax Rate	27.4%	22.6%
LTC Insurance Premiums	$0	$127,100
LTC Benefits Received	$0	~$600,000
Total Lifetime Spending	$4,852,963	$4,852,963

Lifetime spending is identical in both paths. The $973,472 difference, 33 percent more after-tax value for Dash, comes entirely from structural coordination, not better returns or additional savings.

The coordinated plan creates enough structural advantage that Big Red could have increased spending by $20,000 per year during her first eleven years of retirement, a 29 percent increase, and still left Dash approximately what the no-action path would have delivered. The additional spending is funded by lower taxes, better sequencing, and the compounding that coordination preserves. For a plan designed to last twenty-eight years, that flexibility is also how the income system absorbs inflation without breaking the structure underneath it.

IRMAA surcharges were not included in this analysis. The coordinated path pays higher surcharges in the early years because conversion income triggers the threshold sooner. The no-action path avoids surcharges until the mid-seventies but pays them every year thereafter. Net IRMAA cost is modestly higher in the coordinated path. The trade-off is that the coordinated plan eliminates surcharges entirely in the later years. Lowering fixed costs in the future is one of the most effective ways to offset the rising prices inflation has already locked in.

What Actually Changed

Did NOT Change	Did Change
Asset allocation	Order in which income sources were activated
Market returns	Timing and location of tax recognition
Spending levels	Which account funded long-term care, and which was preserved
Investment selection	The marginal rate applied to the final dollars withdrawn and inherited.

The $973,472 improvement did not come from forecasting. It came from treating decisions that look separate as parts of one system.

> **Rule Extracted:**
> Big Red did not fail because she made irrational decisions. She failed because each decision was made independently, often by professionals optimizing only their own piece. The difference between $2.91 million and $3.88 million is not performance. It is architecture.

The Broader Pattern

Acts I, II, and III built the framework. Volatility was managed before it forces a decision. Tax brackets and Roth windows were used before RMDs close them. Income was engineered before account balances dictate what is possible. Big Red is the proof of concept for all of it.

The window to fix these problems closes one year at a time. Unlike the migrations Big Red spent her life tracking, it does not come back around.

Year-by-year cash flows, account balances, Roth conversion schedules, and heir-value projections for both scenarios are detailed in the Appendix.

Ask Your Advisor Today – Big Red Sequence Audit

	Sequence Audit Question
1	Which income source activates first, and has that decision been evaluated in combination with my IRA balance and bracket position, not in isolation?
2	What is the Roth conversion plan during the window before RMDs begin? Has that window been sized, priced, and scheduled?
3	Which tax thresholds matter to my plan: brackets, IRMAA, and Social Security taxation. How are they actively managed?
4	What risks have been transferred off the balance sheet, and at what cost relative to the structural benefit?
5	Who is accountable for the coordination, and how often is the full system reviewed as one plan rather than as separate reports from separate professionals?

ACT IV: The Infrastructure Layer

The first three acts built the fortress around market risk, tax exposure, and inflation. Each of those threats can be modeled, projected, and managed with the tools already in the plan. This act builds the layer underneath.

Infrastructure is capital that can be deployed without disrupting everything else. Accessing liquidity from other sources is costlier than it appears once taxes and secondary consequences are included. A properly designed infrastructure layer creates an alternative: liquidity that arrives without those costs.

When a flexible infrastructure is constructed and coordinated across the plan, it reduces the tax burden and creates the flexibility for every other asset to stay in the role it was designed to fill. Permanent life insurance grows tax-deferred and can be accessed through loans that never appear on a tax return. Long-term care benefits, disability benefits, and death benefits are paid with non-taxable dollars. The tax efficiency is the reason these tools belong in the plan, not on the side of it.

The income that funds the plan is itself at risk. A disability, a care crisis, or a death can each create a deficit the portfolio was never designed to cover. Term insurance replaces the paycheck. Disability coverage keeps the plan funded. Long-term care prevents forced liquidation. Survivorship insurance delivers capital when the estate tax bill arrives. The chapters that follow address each of these as components of one infrastructure layer.

Chapter 10: Long-Term Care: The Risk Most Advisors Avoid, and Why That's Dangerous

Long-term care usually enters the conversation through a parent's crisis.

A client mentions that a parent is receiving in-home care. The details are uncertain. How long will care last. Whether needs will escalate. Whether something temporary is about to become permanent. Then the sentence comes: We never thought it would be like this.

That reaction is common for a reason. According to the Administration for Community Living, someone turning sixty-five today has almost a 70% chance of needing some form of long-term care later in life. Women, on average, need care longer than men, and about 20% of people will need care for longer than five years.

By the time care feels urgent, the best structural options are often gone.

> **Early Decision Rule:**
> If you cannot name the funding source for a multi-year care need, you do not have a plan. You have hope.

The Family Impact Is Often Overlooked

Long-term care affects more than finances. It reshapes family dynamics. Spouses often face reduced financial security, emotional strain, and physical exhaustion. Adult children are pulled into caregiving decisions with little warning and are forced to balance work, children, and responsibility for aging parents. Even when care is provided informally by a spouse, child, or trusted relative, the cost does not disappear. It shifts into lost time, lost income, stress, and reduced independence. Inadequate planning turns families into default insurance policies.

How Long-Term Care Is Defined, and When Benefits Are Triggered

Long-term care is generally defined by functional impairment. Under most policies, benefits are triggered when a licensed health professional certifies that the insured needs assistance with at least two of the six Activities of Daily Living or has cognitive impairment that requires ongoing supervision.

The six Activities of Daily Living are bathing, dressing, eating, transferring, toileting, and continence.

Most policies also require a formal plan of care established by a qualified medical professional.

Medicare is not long-term care insurance. Medicare may cover limited short-term skilled care under specific conditions, but it generally does not cover ongoing custodial care, including most long-term help with daily living activities. Medicaid can cover long-term care, but only after eligibility rules are met and usually with much less choice and control over how care is delivered.

> **Reality Check:**
> Medicare is not the plan. If you do not plan for long-term care, your retirement assets and your family become the default coverage.

Why Long-Term Care Is Structurally Different

Most financial risks are cyclical. Markets recover. Rates normalize. Long-term care risk is different. It is driven by health, longevity, and morbidity, but it requires a financial solution. Costs often rise over time, the duration of care is uncertain, and once the event begins, the financial damage is usually ongoing rather than recoverable.

When no dedicated funding source has been put in place, the portfolio becomes the insurer. That can create higher taxable income, Medicare surcharges, increased Social Security taxation, and forced liquidations when flexibility is already low.

The headline cost is only part of the issue. The deeper planning question is whether care will be funded reactively with after-tax dollars at the worst possible time, or proactively with capital positioned for that purpose. Self-insuring requires more than net worth. It requires liquidity at the right time, assets that can be accessed without forced selling, and cash flow that is not already committed to essential spending.

Long-Term Care Planning Checklist

- **Care setting:** in-home vs assisted living vs skilled nursing.
- **Duration:** baseline three to five years; stress test seven+.
- **Funding order, rank the sources in advance:** cash flow, taxable, IRA, Roth, insurance, home equity.
- **Decision trigger:** when care shifts levels, and who decides.
- **Care floor:** what level must be fundable without derailing the spouse.
- **Role of the house:** sell / borrow / keep.
- **Care inflation assumption:** often higher than CPI, stress test it.

How Long-Term Care Gets Funded

Funding care from IRA withdrawals can increase taxable income, Medicare surcharges, and Social Security taxation. Funding from taxable assets may avoid ordinary income rates but can liquidate assets that might otherwise receive a step-up in basis at death. Roth assets preserve tax efficiency but may be the most valuable dollars to leave untouched. Insurance shifts some or all of the burden to dedicated capital, helping preserve the rest of the plan.

Some households also have specialized options. Existing cash-value insurance may sometimes be repositioned through a tax-free 1035 exchange. HSA dollars may be available for certain qualified medical expenses, and qualified long-term care premiums may receive limited favorable tax treatment depending on age, deduction rules, and policy structure. The rules vary enough that these decisions should be coordinated with both an advisor and a CPA.

From Traditional Policies to Modern Solutions

Traditional long-term care insurance developed a poor reputation for understandable reasons. Policies were often mispriced, premiums rose sharply over time, and many seniors were priced out of coverage just when they were most likely to need it. The need for planning did not disappear. The solutions changed.

Hybrid policies integrate long-term care benefits with either life insurance or annuity structures. The job is to prevent a care event from turning into forced selling, forced income, and a surviving-spouse plan that breaks under stress. These designs can allow care at home, in facilities, or through informal caregivers. Benefit amounts, duration, and inflation features are selected up front, creating more clarity and control.

Many policies are built with modest initial benefits and inflation riders, so coverage grows over time and peaks when care is most likely to be needed.

Cash-indemnity designs can also reduce administrative friction by paying benefits based on qualification rather than only through reimbursement receipts.

Most important, many modern structures preserve value even if care is never needed. Benefits may be paid as care, as a death benefit, or through retained contract value. That addresses the "use it or lose it" objection that damaged confidence in older policy designs.

Murray: What Self-Insurance Actually Costs

Murray came home from the war with little except a willingness to work. He started delivering eggs for a farm in Connecticut. Over thirty years, he saved enough to buy the chicken farm, expanded it, and sold the business for a price that reflected everything he had put into it. He accumulated quite a nest egg.

He retired at sixty-five with $6,000,000 in a qualified retirement plan growing at 7.5 percent annually, $100,000 in annual installment payments from the business sale, and Social Security of $42,900 beginning at seventy. He needed an additional $150,000 post tax from his IRA to meet his living expenses.

His advisor told him he was wealthy enough to self-insure long-term care. Murray agreed. He could afford the care. What nobody modeled was what self-insuring would cost his daughter Sonia.

Starting at seventy-three, RMDs exceeded his spending needs. The after-tax surplus flowed into a taxable brokerage account. At eighty-five, Murray developed dementia and moved into memory care at $240,000 a year for six years. His RMDs, taxed at a combined federal and Connecticut rate of 43.99 percent, covered care and living expenses. Murray's bills were paid.

At sixty, Murray could have purchased a hybrid long-term care policy for $16,000 a year over ten years, $160,000 total. The policy would have produced approximately $1,440,000 of tax-free benefits during the care event. Without insurance, care costs were absorbed by the excess RMDs, reducing what accumulated in the brokerage account.

Sonia, a New York City resident, faced a combined tax rate of approximately 52 percent on inherited retirement assets. The brokerage passed with a step-up in basis with no income tax at death. The retirement plan passed as ordinary income at her full marginal rate.

	No Insurance	Long-Term Care Insurance	Difference
Retirement plan to Sonia (after 52% income tax)	$5,688,714	$5,338,120	−$350,594
Brokerage to Sonia (no tax at death)	$3,110,220	$4,221,327	+$1,111,107
Total after-tax estate to Sonia	$8,798,935	$9,559,447	+$760,513
Estate increase			+8.64%

Note: Simplified illustration. Model output based on RMD schedule, and assumptions in the narrative.

The $160,000 in premiums Murray did not pay cost Sonia $760,513. The investments grew at the same rate. Spending was the same. The only difference was which account absorbed the cost of care. Murray's advisor was not watching the entire nest. He was watching the eggs he was responsible for. He never noticed that some were cracking.

Rule Extracted:
The decision to self-insure is not made in isolation. Every dollar of care funded from the wrong account at the wrong tax rate is a dollar permanently removed from the estate. Murray did not have a resource problem. He had a design problem.

Planning for Dignity and Control

Long-term care planning is about more than cost. It is about preserving dignity, control, and the ability to choose where care is delivered, who provides it, and how the burden is shared. A funded plan preserves those choices. An unfunded plan usually does not.

Not making a decision is still a decision. The cost of care, the tax consequences, and the burden of caregiving remain with the family.

The next chapter addresses the income that funds every other part of the plan, and what happens when it stops. Whether the interruption comes from a disability or a death, the question is the same: does the plan keep working without the paycheck that built it?

Ask Your Advisor Today – Long-Term Care
Benefit design: If we choose insurance, what specific benefit structure is being engineered, and what risk is intentionally left to self-fund?
Spouse impact: In a three, five, and seven-year care scenario, show the specific effect on my spouse's retirement income and the estate plan.
Self-insurance cost: If I self-insure a long-term care event, which account funds it first? What is the after-tax cost of that decision to my heir, at their tax rate?

Chapter 11: The Protection Layer: Term, Disability, and the Coverage Most Plans Get Wrong

Most financial plans do not fail because markets decline. They fail when the income funding the plan disappears. Term insurance protects against premature death while others still depend on that income. Disability insurance protects against a more prolonged risk. Income stops while expenses continue. Together, they form the protection layer that the rest of the plan depends on.

Term insurance is usually the cleanest tool for temporary risks: financially dependent children, a large mortgage, or a household relying heavily on one earner. It is a temporary solution to a temporary problem. Its design comes down to two decisions: how much protection is needed and how long that need is likely to last. Common terms are ten, fifteen, twenty, and thirty years. Premiums are generally fixed during the selected term, and coverage ends when the term expires. Cost is driven primarily by age, sex, and health classification. Underwriting classes vary by carrier and can change pricing substantially. The same applicant can receive different ratings and different premiums from different insurers, which makes carrier selection a planning decision, not a formality.

One feature is especially favorable: life-insurance death benefits are generally received income-tax free by beneficiaries, which makes term insurance one of the most tax-efficient forms of income replacement available.

Mama Starr Structures Term Life Policies

Mama Starr is a thirty-eight-year-old architect with a simple professional philosophy: every structure she designs should function as a fortress, solid on paper and stronger still when conditions turn against it. She and her husband have three children: Avery, age twelve; Jolie, age seven; and Mark, age two. Mama Starr wants coverage that replaces her income for the next twenty years, pays off a twenty-year mortgage, and funds college through age twenty-two for each child.

Income-replacement needs do not stay constant. Every year Mama Starr remains alive, another year of earnings has already been produced, the mortgage is smaller, and fewer years of childcare and education remain. College costs also happen on a schedule: Avery's window ends first, then Jolie's, then Mark's. A single twenty-year policy sized for the maximum need treats all years as if they carry the same obligations.

A more precise strategy is to ladder multiple policies, so coverage declines as obligations decline. Instead of buying one large policy for the full period, coverage can be split across ten-year, fifteen-year, and twenty-year terms.

Term Insurance: Single Policy vs. Laddered Structure

	Single 20-Year Policy	Laddered (10/15/20)
Coverage at year 1	$3,000,000	$3,000,000
Coverage at year 11	$3,000,000	$2,000,000
Coverage at year 16	$3,000,000	$1,000,000
Annual premium (years 1–10)	$1,425	$1,260
Annual premium (years 11–15)	$1,425	$935
Annual premium (years 16–20)	$1,425	$525
Total premiums over 20 years	**$28,500**	**$19,900**
Premium savings		**$8,600 (30%)**

38-year-old female, preferred health classification. Premiums are illustrative and will vary by carrier, underwriting, and health status.

The single policy pays for $3,000,000 of coverage in year sixteen when only $1,000,000 of obligation remains. Avery is done with college. Jolie is done. The mortgage is smaller. The only child still in the window is Mark. The laddered approach reduces coverage as obligations decline, saving $8,600 in total premiums over twenty years. Paying for protection the family no longer needs is a waste.

Mama Starr had been laddering structures her entire career. She had never thought to ladder her insurance.

When Term Isn't Enough

Death is a single moment. Disability is a timeline: months, years, and sometimes permanently, during which expenses continue and often increase while choices narrow. Disability is also more common than most households assume. At many working ages, the probability of disability exceeds the probability of premature death. That matters because earned income funds everything else: living expenses, debt service, retirement savings, and even other insurance premiums.

How Disability Coverage Actually Works

Tax treatment is frequently misunderstood, and it matters enormously. Individually owned disability policies are typically funded with after-tax dollars, and benefits are generally income-tax free. Employer-sponsored plans are often funded by the employer or through pre-tax arrangements, which usually makes benefits taxable when they are paid. A group plan promising sixty percent income replacement may deliver significantly less after tax than the headline suggests. When evaluating how much disability coverage is needed, the after-tax replacement rate is the number that matters.

The most consequential provision is often not the benefit amount or the premium. It is the definition of disability.

Own occupation coverage pays if the insured cannot perform the material duties of their specific occupation, even if they can work in another field. A surgeon who loses fine motor control can still qualify while teaching or consulting.

Any occupation coverage is narrower. It generally pays only if the insured cannot perform any occupation reasonably suited to education, training, or experience.

Many group plans begin with a more favorable definition and later become stricter, sometimes after twenty-four months. That transition is often the most financially dangerous part of the contract. For many high earners, the definition clause is the most important line in the policy.

Most individual policies begin paying after a ninety-day elimination period and should extend benefits at least to age sixty-five. Three riders are worth reviewing with an advisor: residual or partial disability benefits, future increase options, and cost-of-living adjustments.

The Self-Insurance Trap

Many high earners assume accumulated assets make disability insurance unnecessary. The problem extends beyond replacing income. A disability can arrive with higher medical costs, changes to housing or transportation, and reduced flexibility in how the household earns or spends. At the same time, retirement contributions stop, compounding is interrupted, and the years available to rebuild are reduced.

Self-insuring that risk requires more than a strong balance sheet. It requires enough liquid capital to replace years of income, absorb higher expenses, and preserve the rest of the plan without derailing retirement. That threshold is much higher than most households carry during their peak earning years.

Early Decision Rule:
The cost of true own-occupation disability coverage is often only a small percentage of take-home pay. The benefit is protecting income if you can no longer do your actual job. It is a structural decision.

Lox's Disability: The Definition Risk

Lox is the lead singer of The Orange Herrings, a regional rock band that finally made it after fifteen years of touring, licensing deals, and a loyal following. At forty-three, he permanently lost his voice. The official cause was a rare vocal-cord condition. The rumor is that he lost it somewhere between Altuna and Scrodton while eating too much gefilte fish. Either way, he cannot sing, and he never will again.

The band's contract includes group long-term disability coverage: sixty percent income replacement on his $200,000 income, with a more favorable occupation definition for twenty-four months and a stricter one after that. Lox always assumed he was covered. He had never looked closely at the definition clause.

	Employer-Paid Only	Employer + Private Own-Occupation
Working income (after-tax)	$152,200	$152,200
Annual premium	$0	$2,200
Take-home after premium	$152,200 (100%)	$150,000 (98.5%)
If Disabled:		
After-tax income (Years 1-2)	$106,800 (70%)	$146,800 (96%)
After-tax income (Years 3+ if able to work elsewhere)	$78,000 (51%)	$118,000 (77%)
Coverage definition	Any-occupation after 24 months	True own-occupation to age 65

Simplified illustration. Employer-paid benefits treated as taxable; individual-policy benefits treated as tax-free when premiums are paid with after-tax dollars. Actual results depend on policy terms, offsets, and tax rules.

Then the definition changes after twenty-four months.

The insurer no longer asks whether Lox can do his job. It asks whether he can do any job reasonably suited to his background. If Lox remains disabled from all work, both plans keep paying and household income stays close to the Years 1–2 level.

The more dangerous outcome is narrower. Lox is still disabled from singing but can work in another capacity. He is not cognitively impaired. He is simply unable to perform the specific role he spent twenty years building. The group plan terminates.

Lox eventually finds work as the frontman of a local lip-sync cover band performing the music of Fish. There is no need to use his voice. The irony is not lost on him. Salary: $95,000. After tax: about $78,000. His household went from roughly $152,200 after tax to $78,000. That is for the next twenty years.

For $2,200 a year, about 1.5 percent of his take-home pay, Lox could have supplemented the group plan with a private true own-occupation policy equal to twenty percent of income, or $40,000 a year. Because the supplemental private policy was purchased with after-tax dollars, the $40,000 benefit is generally not taxed. The purpose of the private policy is to supplement the employer benefit and preserve the stronger definition of disability. In that narrower outcome, after the group plan shifted to any-occupation and terminated, the private policy could still have paid because Lox remained unable to perform his actual occupation, even after returning to work in another capacity. That preserved a much larger share of household income after the group definition tightened.

Disability insurance keeps the household intact if a disability occurs. The plan that survives a disability is the one that transferred the risk before it arrived, not the one that assumed it would not. Term and disability protect what is still being built. Permanent life insurance addresses a different set of problems: liquidity, survivor stability, and transfer. That is where the next chapter begins.

Ask Your Advisor Today – The Protection Layer

Net replacement: If I become disabled, what is my after-tax monthly income from all sources, and how long does it last?

Contract definition: Do I have true own-occupation coverage for the full benefit period, or does the definition become more restrictive after two years?

Life insurance amount: How was my life-insurance need calculated, and what specific obligations is it meant to cover: income replacement, mortgage payoff, education funding, estate liquidity, or something else?

Chapter 12: Insurance as Infrastructure

> **Early Decision Rule:**
> A plan can be strong on paper and still fail without infrastructure to support it. A death, a care crisis, a business transition, or an estate obligation can each create immediate liquidity needs that other tools cannot absorb. That is what infrastructure solves.

Where that liquidity comes from determines the cost. Selling securities triggers taxes. Withdrawing from retirement accounts increases brackets and Medicare premiums. Borrowing creates debt service on a fixed income. Infrastructure creates a fourth option: capital that can be accessed without any of those consequences.

> **Reality Check:**
> Wealth alone does not create continuity. Liquidity must be there when it is needed, or the rest of the plan starts to unravel.

Beyond the Death Benefit

When most people think of insurance, they think of the death benefit. Term insurance addresses that risk efficiently as discussed in Chapter 11.

Permanent insurance uses the same mechanism, but that is rarely its most important role. A properly structured permanent contract supports continuity by creating tax-advantaged liquidity, reducing the need to sell assets under pressure, and preserving flexibility across major transitions. That value only exists if the contract is structured for the job.

How Cash-Value Life Insurance Functions as Infrastructure

A properly structured cash-value policy creates a pool of capital that grows tax-deferred and can be accessed through policy loans without triggering a taxable event. The alternative is selling securities or withdrawing from a retirement account. Either creates tax consequences, disrupts compounding, and may force a sale at a distressed price.

A policy loan works differently from a bank loan. The insurer uses the policy itself as collateral. There is no credit check, no repayment schedule, and no required monthly payment. Interest accrues against the policy. If the loan is never repaid, the outstanding balance reduces the death benefit when the claim is paid. The policy remains in force as long as the cash value supports it.

That structure has a specific tax consequence: nothing. The loan does not appear on a tax return, does not affect brackets, does not trigger IRMAA surcharges, and does not increase the taxable portion of Social Security. The result depends on policy structure, MEC status, and loan management — but when managed correctly, this is liquidity without the friction that accompanies every other source in the plan.

The applications are broad and covered in the Act IV capstone. The principle is simple: capital that arrives without a tax bill is more versatile than capital that does not.

Survivorship Insurance and Estate Timing

Survivorship life insurance, or second-to-die insurance, is used when the main liquidity need arises only after both spouses have died, most commonly for estate taxes, dependent support, or beneficiary equalization. The death benefit is paid at the second death, which aligns the contract with the timing of those obligations.

That timing also explains why survivorship insurance is often less expensive. The insurer pays the benefit at the second death, which always occurs later than the first death. With more years of premium and/or growth, the same death benefit can be purchased at a lower cost than with two separate traditional policies.

Lower premium cost, matched timing, and aligned structure. That is what makes survivorship insurance useful infrastructure rather than a generic product.

Designing a Policy for Infrastructure

A permanent contract balances death benefit with cash value growth. Where that balance is set determines what the policy can do. If too much premium is paid relative to the death benefit, the policy becomes a Modified Endowment Contract and loses its tax-advantaged access. Structuring below that threshold, with minimum insurance costs and maximum allowable funding, builds cash value that can be accessed through tax-exempt loans. That is the infrastructure a well-designed plan needs.

Most planning needs evolve. A structure that cannot adapt becomes a cost rather than an asset. When a policy no longer aligns with its current objective, repositioning can allow accumulated value to move into a new structure without current tax consequences. That is a planning decision, not a product change, and should be evaluated with an advisor.

The next act shifts from financial protection to governance: who controls the plan, who can execute it, and whether the legal structure around the wealth is strong enough to keep the fortress standing when the original decision-maker is no longer there.

Ask Your Advisor Today – Insurance as Infrastructure
Infrastructure role: What specific continuity problem is each insurance contract solving: survivor liquidity, estate liquidity, business continuity, dependent support, or equalization, is the current structure the most efficient way to solve it?
Structure review: Is the current contract the most efficient structure for what it's meant to do, or has the objective changed?
Ownership and control: Who owns the policy, who receives the proceeds, and does that structure support or undermine the intended tax and estate outcome?

Integration Check: Act IV: Protecting the Plan

1. Which risks are intentionally insured? Which are implicitly self-insured by the portfolio?
2. If a major life event disrupted the plan tomorrow, where would liquidity come from, who has authority to act, and what would remain intact for my spouse, dependents, and estate?
3. Is there a single uncoordinated decision in my current plan: an insurance gap, an account structure, a withdrawal sequence, that, if it goes wrong, forces a bad outcome somewhere else?

ACT IV CAPSTONE: Isidore's Infrastructure

Isidore: Designing the Policy for the Job

Isidore owns a shoe factory. A workaholic by any measure, he built his reputation on loafers, which is quite ironic. At fifty, with the business on solid footing and his income in the highest marginal bracket, he sits down to review an insurance policy purchased a decade ago. The policy carries a $1.9 million death benefit, structured for maximum death benefit. It no longer fits the job the contract needs to do.

Why Maximum Death Benefit Was the Wrong Structure

There are legitimate reasons to maximize a permanent policy's death benefit: business succession, estate-tax liquidity, trust funding, or survivorship planning. A forty-year-old starting a business is not automatically in one of those categories. If the objective at forty was maximum death-benefit protection, the cleanest answer was term insurance.

Isidore's original policy committed $15,000 per year for thirty years at maximum death benefit. The structure directed too much of each premium dollar toward insurance charges and too little toward cash-value growth. Flexibility was limited. If Isidore ever needed to miss a payment because of business disruption, the policy had little cushion. The feature that makes permanent insurance worth owning long term, tax-advantaged accumulation, was starved from the start.

The Same Premium, Two Different Outcomes
The same $15,000 annual premium, paid over thirty years, produces dramatically different results by age seventy-five depending on how the death benefit is set.

Policy Structure	Initial Death Benefit	Cash Value at 75	Death Benefit at 75
Max Non-MEC contract	$675,647	$1,507,454	$1,909,144
Max Death Benefit contract	$1,904,556	$826,763	$1,904,556

Hypothetical illustration assuming 6.47% average annual index return before policy charges. Actual performance will depend on caps, participation rates, fees, and policy design. Not a guarantee of results. Premium: $15,000 per year for 30 years in both scenarios.

The death benefit at seventy-five is virtually identical: $1,909,144 versus $1,904,556. The cash value is not. The Max Non-MEC structure produces $1,507,454 in accessible, tax-advantaged capital. For functionally the same death benefit at age seventy-five, the maximum-death-benefit structure sacrificed $680,691 in cash value.

During the thirty-five years before age seventy-five, the maximum-death-benefit policy does provide more death protection if Isidore dies early. But that is the wrong chassis for that job. A 40-year-old male in standard health can purchase $1,300,000 of twenty-year term insurance for approximately $1,475 per year. Term handles early death protection efficiently. Separating the two jobs from the start creates the $680,691 in flexible, tax-advantaged capital that makes the policy worth owning for the next thirty-five years.

The Better Structure: Blend Term and Permanent

Isidore's $15,000 annual budget does not need to change. What needs to change is how it is allocated. Term insurance handles death-benefit protection efficiently during working years. The permanent contract handles long-term accumulation. The same dollars, split across two products built for their respective jobs, produce better results in both dimensions.

Alternative: 20-Year Term + Max Non-MEC (with Premium Redirect)

Policy	Annual Premium	Initial Death Benefit	Cash Value at 75	Death Benefit at 75
20-year term	$1,475	$1,300,000	N/A	N/A
Max Non-MEC contract	$13,525 (ages 40–60)	$610,000	$1,383,100	$1,751,729
	$25,280 (ages 61–65)			
Combined	$15,000	$1,910,000	$1,383,100	$1,751,729

Redirects the expiring term premium into the permanent contract at ages 61–65, increasing annual funding to $25,280 for five years. Same $15,000 total annual outlay throughout. Hypothetical 6% average annual index return before policy charges. Not a guarantee of results.

After the term expires, Isidore's options expand rather than narrow: buy additional coverage if still needed, reduce premiums, or let the permanent contract's death benefit grow alongside the cash value. That flexibility is the point, and it only exists because the structure was built for it.

The blended structure produced $556,337 more in cash value than the max-death-benefit alternative. The death benefit at seventy-five is $152,827 lower, a modest trade-off for more than half a million dollars in flexible, tax-advantaged capital. That capital is infrastructure, positioned to solve whatever problem arrives next.

What the Infrastructure Made Possible

What follows are four scenarios. Each one is a different version of Isidore's life after sixty-five. Same policy. Same premium history. Different demands. The point is not which path is best. The point is that the infrastructure supported all four.

Scenario 1: Business Expansion at Sixty-Six
The shoe factory needed capital. Isidore saw an opportunity to expand into a second facility. The cost was $1,000,000. A bank would have required underwriting, collateral, covenants, and monthly payments that would stress the business during a growth phase.

Isidore borrowed $1,000,000 from the policy instead. No bank approval. No business assets pledged. No taxable event. Interest accrued against the policy rather than requiring monthly payments, preserving business cash flow during the expansion.

The factory expanded. The business grew. And the balance sheet never showed a dollar of bank debt.

Scenario 2: Roth Conversion Bridge at Sixty-Six
Isidore sold the business and stepped back. His income dropped. His bracket dropped with it. This was the conversion window; the years when IRA dollars could move to Roth at the lowest rates he would ever see.

The problem was cash flow. Living expenses and conversion taxes had to come from somewhere, and pulling from the IRA to pay conversion taxes defeats the purpose. Pulling from the brokerage triggers gains.

The policy solved both. From sixty-six through seventy-two, Isidore took $120,000 per year in policy loans, $840,000 over seven years. That income did not appear on a tax return. No bracket impact. No IRMAA trigger. No Social Security taxation. The IRA dollars flowed into Roth at the lowest rates available, and the bridge that made it possible was invisible to the tax code.

At the end of the conversion window, the policy still carried a $250,000 death benefit. The Roth was built. The tax bill was controlled. And the bridge cost nothing in taxes.

Scenario 3: Partner Buyout at Eighty
Decades earlier, Isidore had brought in a partner to help grow the factory. By eighty, the partnership had run its course. His children wanted full ownership. The buyout price was $1,650,000.

A bank loan at eighty was unattractive, the terms, the underwriting, and the monthly payments on a fixed retirement income. Selling portfolio assets would trigger capital gains and disturb assets heading toward a step-up in basis for his heirs.

Isidore accessed $1,650,000 from the policy. No bank. No taxable event. No portfolio disruption. His beneficiaries gained sole ownership of the business, and the transfer happened on Isidore's terms rather than a lender's.

Scenario 4: Leave It Alone
Life cooperated. The business stayed healthy. Income was sufficient. Care never arrived. Isidore never touched the policy.

At 90, the death benefit had grown to $3,671,157. That amount transferred to his beneficiaries, income-tax-free, outside probate, and immediately available when liquidity mattered most.

The policy compounded for fifty years. That was the point. It was there if needed and worth more because it was never needed.

See Appendix Disclosures.

What the Infrastructure Actually Proved

Four scenarios. Four different versions of life. Same $15,000 annual premium chosen at age forty.

The original max-death-benefit structure could do one thing, pay at death. This structure served as a private credit facility for business expansion, a tax-invisible bridge for Roth conversions, a buyout mechanism that preserved family ownership, and a $3.67 million tax-free estate transfer. Each solution would have otherwise required selling assets, triggering taxes, taking bank debt, or depleting the retirement portfolio.

None of these scenarios were known at age forty. All of them were addressed by a structure built for flexibility rather than a single purpose. That is the difference between a product and infrastructure.

> **Rule Extracted:**
> Insurance becomes infrastructure when the structure supports multiple jobs across a lifetime. A policy designed for one moment cannot serve a life that changes. A policy designed for flexibility can.

Ask Your Advisor Today – Isidore Capstone

Structure audit: For every permanent policy I own, is the structure aligned with the job it needs to do today, or the job it was purchased for years ago?

Infrastructure test: If I needed $500,000 in liquidity tomorrow for a: buyout, care event, conversion window, or opportunity, where would it come from, and what would it cost in taxes and disruption?

Flexibility inventory: How many of the problems my plan might face in the next twenty years can be addressed by the infrastructure already in place, and how many would require selling assets or taking debt?

ACT V: Control and Continuity

By this point, the fortress is largely built. Market exposure has been engineered for stress, taxes and account structures are coordinated, income is designed, and major risks are insured or transferred. Act V adds the final layer: governance. It focuses on the legal framework, survivor continuity, and advisor oversight that keep the fortress stable when you are no longer the one making the decisions, during incapacity, after a spouse dies, and across the transition to heirs.

Chapter 13: Estate Planning as Retirement Control During Life and Transition

Retirement planning assumes you remain the decision-maker. Estate planning exists because eventually, you will not.

> **Early Decision Rule**:
> Estate planning is governance: who can act, what is accessible, and how decisions get made when you cannot act.

For retirees, estate planning is about operational continuity: who pays bills and manages accounts during incapacity, who makes medical decisions without court involvement, what happens to retirement income if the decision-maker cannot manage distributions and Social Security logistics, and where liquidity comes from for final expenses and taxes without forcing a sale into a down market.

The strategic purpose is operational control during the transition years, when authority weakens, timing matters, and the surviving spouse is under pressure.

Estate Planning Is Three Systems:
1) **Control while alive:** powers of attorney, healthcare directives, trustees, and account access
2) **Transfer at death:** beneficiary designations, titling, and trust terms
3) **Taxes and liquidity:** settlement costs, income disruption, and funding sources that prevent forced sales

Many retirees delay because the risk feels distant or because their net worth appears below estate-tax thresholds. That logic fails for retirement households. Incapacity does not arrive on a schedule. Family dynamics change. Laws evolve. Market timing is unpredictable. Planning is about retaining decision authority and liquidity when conditions are least forgiving.

Ignoring these questions does not eliminate them. It defers them to the moment when options are narrower and emotions are higher.

Probate, Delay, and the Cost of Inaction

For retirees, the most expensive feature of probate is the delay.

Probate is not inherently punitive, but it often slows access to accounts, reduces flexibility, and forces families into administrative steps at the moment they need speed. Paying bills. Stabilizing income. Making decisions under stress.

When a financial institution receives notice of death, accounts held solely in the deceased person's name may be restricted until the right legal authority and documentation are provided. The specific procedures, timelines, and costs vary by state. The core problem does not: delay arrives when the household and portfolio are least equipped to tolerate it.

> **Reality Check:**
> Probate creates delay at the worst time. Accounts can be restricted, decisions can slow, and flexibility can disappear when the family most needs speed.

Harry and Pauline's Justice: Equalizing an Unequal Retirement Estate

After thirty years of clocking in, Harry and Pauline finally had time on their hands. Harry's lifelong hobby was collecting and restoring antique timepieces. The collection started with pieces relatives smuggled over from the old country and expanded through decades of estate sales across the state. At fifty-five, Pauline was pleased they had something to share facing a long retirement.

Both were police officers. Their salaries never afforded much savings, but between pensions and Social Security they had more than enough to live on. The problem was what they owned. The family home and the collection were valuable, appreciating, and impossible to split.

They had three children. Rose wanted the house. Philip treated the collection as his own. Ephraim had no interest in either. No one could predict what the home or collection would be worth when Harry and Pauline's time was up. As police officers, they wanted justice and equal treatment for their children. Without a plan, an equal split would require selling the house, liquidating the collection, or both, possibly at discounted prices. Grief would arrive with a negotiation attached.

Harry and Pauline needed to solve a problem that would only matter after both of them were gone.

At fifty-five, they purchased a survivorship life insurance policy with a $1,500,000 death benefit and an annual premium of $15,000 funded from pension income. The policy was owned by an irrevocable life insurance trust, keeping the proceeds outside the taxable estate and available immediately at the second death.

At the second death, the trustee distributed the insurance proceeds to equalize the shares regardless of what the illiquid assets had appreciated to by that point. Rose received the house. Philip received the collection. Ephraim received cash. No forced sale. No strained relationships. No negotiation during grief.

The survivorship policy was infrastructure. It provided liquidity the estate did not have, equalized shares that existing assets could not, and arrived at the second death when the obligation existed. The irrevocable trust kept the proceeds outside the estate, protected from creditors, and accessible without probate delay. Assets went to the right people in the right form. The cost of the policy was predictable. The cost of not having it would have been determined by grief, time pressure, and a market nobody controls.

Decision Authority: Living Wills and Powers

A spouse or adult child may know exactly what you want. Without legal authority, they may be unable to act. They cannot pay bills, move money, coordinate care, or speak with institutions on your behalf. Durable powers of attorney and healthcare directives are the operating permissions for your retirement plan when you cannot operate it. Healthcare directives preserve dignity. Financial powers preserve continuity. Review both regularly. Family dynamics change, agents age, and an outdated document can paralyze even a well-funded estate.

The goal is operational continuity. The surviving spouse needs to execute a plan without court involvement, forced selling, or confusion. Chapter 14 builds that framework from the survivor's perspective.

Beneficiary Designations, Titling, and Retirement Accounts

Many estate plans fail because the documents say one thing and the assets do another.

Many of the most valuable assets pass by contract or title, not by will. IRAs, life insurance, annuities, payable-on-death accounts, and jointly titled assets all bypass the will entirely. Those mechanisms control who receives the asset and how quickly it moves, regardless of what the broader documents intended. Your estate plan is the documents, plus beneficiary forms, plus titling. All three need to match.

For many retirees, the largest "estate asset" is the IRA or 401(k). That means beneficiary decisions are not a formality. They shape control, income continuity, and the survivor's tax picture.

If the account is meant to support the surviving spouse's lifestyle, the design usually should prioritize access, simplicity, and flexibility for that spouse first. If the goal is to protect a vulnerable heir, that is usually a trust conversation, but the beneficiary form still has to reflect that intent.

Design Choice Checkpoint:
Beneficiary forms and account titling can override the practical result the will was meant to achieve, so they need to match the retirement income plan.

Revocable Trusts: Control Without Commitment

For many retirees, the primary value of a revocable living trust is continuity.

Not tax savings. Continuity.

A revocable living trust can help avoid probate for assets actually titled to the trust and can create continuity during incapacity by naming who steps in to manage those trust-owned assets. Its main retirement value is reduced friction: fewer court delays, clearer authority, and a smoother handoff for the surviving spouse. But the document alone is not enough. To produce probate-avoidance benefits, the trust generally must be funded by retitling assets into the trust or making them payable to it where appropriate.

Some families need structures beyond it: irrevocable trusts for estate-tax exposure, special needs trusts for disabled beneficiaries, or spendthrift provisions for at-risk heirs. If any of those apply, treat it as specialist legal work and coordinate it with the retirement income plan before the documents are drafted.

Legal documents establish authority. They do not eliminate interpretation. Once control passes from the original decision-maker to other people, the estate plan becomes a human system as much as a legal one.

Governance Is Human Before It Is Legal

Many estate plans are drafted as if the only variable is the tax code. In real families, the larger variable is interpretation.

> **Reality Check:**
> People rarely fight over dollars. They fight over meaning.

A distribution is rarely experienced as just money. It gets interpreted as respect, trust, favoritism, obligation, or abandonment. Especially when communication has been vague.

> **Design Choice Checkpoint:**
> Unequal requires a narrative. Equal is simple. Fairness is subjective.

As circumstances diverge through caregiving, health needs, financial risk, or prior support, unequal planning without explanation invites resentment and conflict.

A letter of intent, sometimes called a letter of wishes or instruction, adds context for the executor or trustee. It is not legally binding. It explains why the plan is structured the way it is, what you want the money to accomplish, who you chose as executor or trustee and why, and what "fair" means in your family. It should be kept consistent with the legal documents, stored with the estate binder or continuity file, and updated when family circumstances change.

Trustee selection is also a human decision. Trustworthiness is necessary. It is not sufficient. Trustees also need competence, time, emotional independence, and the willingness to say no. They have duties to communicate, to act impartially, and to keep process moving when other family members may be emotional or reactive. If those traits do not exist inside the family, a professional trustee can be a governance tool, not a family judgment.

Preparing heirs is part of the plan. Trusts can enforce timing. They cannot create maturity. The best outcomes usually come when expectations are aligned while you are still alive. Adult children do not need every dollar disclosed, but they usually do need clarity about roles, process, and intent: who will act, why decisions were made the way they were, what "fair" means in your family, and what responsibilities come with inheritance.

You do not need to negotiate. You do need to communicate.

Taxes, Liquidity, and Control

Estate planning is inseparable from taxation, but taxes should not be the only lens.

The key trade-off is governance. Moving assets out of your estate may reduce transfer-tax exposure, but it often comes at the cost of control and flexibility. In retirement, the decision rule is simple: do not pursue tax savings that reduce the surviving spouse's access to cash, decision authority, or operational simplicity.

Liquidity prevents forced sales, stabilizes the surviving spouse, and buys time. Cash at death can pay immediate bills, cover final expenses, support the survivor while accounts are being transferred, and prevent a concentrated or illiquid portfolio from being sold under pressure.

Life-insurance death benefits are generally received income-tax free by beneficiaries under federal law, subject to limited exceptions. Tax-free cash at death solves problems that portfolios and illiquid assets cannot solve.

Control Is the Core of Any Infrastructure

Authority, liquidity, and structure determine whether your plan functions during transition or becomes a court process, a tax problem, or a forced-sale problem. Control is the outcome. The surviving spouse needs to be able to exercise it, and Chapter 14 is written for exactly that moment.

Ask Your Advisor Today – Estate Planning
Authority and access: If I became incapacitated tomorrow, who has legal authority to act, and will institutions recognize those documents without delay?
Alignment audit: Are beneficiary designations and account titling coordinated with the trust plan? Show me the inventory.
Survivor impact: If I died this month, what changes for the surviving spouse: income, filing status, account access, and Medicare premiums, shown together in one number?

Chapter 14: Survivor Continuity, What the Surviving Spouse Needs to Know

Most estate plans are written for the person making the decisions. This chapter is for the person left behind.

> **Early Decision Rule:**
> First 90 days. The goal is not optimization. It is avoiding irreversible mistakes while grief is fresh and information is incomplete.

The worst time to learn how a plan works is the day it has to be executed.

The First Seventy-Two Hours: Stability Before Strategy

The first seventy-two hours are not about strategy. They are about stability.

Three priorities matter immediately:

- Call the coordinator
- Access to cash
- Authority to act

Someone to Call

Every survivor needs one coordinator who understands how the pieces connect. That may be the advisor, attorney, CPA, or a well-briefed family member. The role is simple: direct traffic in the first week.

That person should know where the documents are, who holds the originals, which institutions need to be contacted, and who is responsible for what.

Immediate Cash Access

Bills do not pause for grief. Mortgage payments, utilities, insurance premiums, and ordinary household expenses continue.

The surviving spouse needs to know:

- which accounts are jointly titled and accessible now
- where the primary checking account is held, and whether they already have signing authority
- which credit cards are in their own name, and which were in the deceased spouse's name alone
- whether any automatic payments could fail if an individually titled account becomes restricted

Accounts titled solely in the deceased spouse's name may be restricted once the institution is notified of death. Joint accounts with rights of survivorship are often more accessible, depending on titling and the institution's procedures.

A practical rule: identify at least 90 days of liquid funds that can be accessed without court action, account transfers, or selling investments.

Authority to Act

Three documents determine who can do what:

- the **will**, which names the executor responsible for administering the estate
- the **revocable trust**, if one exists, which names the successor trustee who can act for trust-owned assets
- **beneficiary designations**, which control retirement accounts, life insurance, and annuities

If you are the executor or successor trustee, you may have authority to act. If someone else is named, you need to know who that is and how to reach them. The coordinator from the first section can help locate that information quickly.

The First Thirty Days: Notification and Documentation

The administrative burden of death is substantial. These tasks cannot be eliminated, but they can be organized.

Obtain Death Certificates
You will need more certified copies than you expect. Most institutions require certified copies, not photocopies. In practice, it is often wise to order ten to fifteen.

Common uses include:

- banks and brokerages
- retirement account custodians
- insurance companies
- the Social Security Administration
- pension administrators
- real estate title transfers
- vehicle title transfers

Priority Notifications in the First Thirty Days
Social Security Administration: Report the death, stop benefits where required, and ask about survivor benefits. If both spouses were receiving Social Security, the smaller benefit stops. If one spouse had not yet claimed, survivor benefits may be available and may exceed the survivor's own retirement benefit.
Life insurance companies: File claims promptly. Many policies pay within thirty to sixty days after a complete claim submission. Delays are usually caused by missing documentation, not by coverage disputes.
Employer, if applicable: Ask about final paychecks, accrued benefits, employer life insurance, pension options, and COBRA continuation coverage if the survivor was on the deceased spouse's health plan.
Financial institutions: Notify banks and brokerages, then ask three direct questions:

- what is restricted now

- what remains accessible
- what documents are required next

Assemble the Document Inventory
Before making decisions, gather:

- the most recent will and any codicils
- trust documents
- beneficiary designation records for retirement accounts and insurance policies
- recent tax returns, ideally the last three years
- investment account statements
- insurance policy declarations or summaries
- property deeds and vehicle titles

The person who understands the plan should already know where these documents are. If not, that is a continuity gap.

Days Thirty-Ninety: Decisions That Cannot Wait, and Decisions That Can

Grief distorts judgment. Survivors act too quickly on decisions that can wait and delay decisions that carry deadlines.

Decisions That Cannot Wait
Health insurance continuation: COBRA and related health-coverage elections are time-sensitive. Missing the election window can leave the survivor uninsured with no immediate alternative.
Retirement account elections: A surviving spouse often has options that other beneficiaries do not, including treating an IRA as their own through a spousal rollover or keeping it as an inherited IRA. The right choice depends on age, income needs, and timing. Large withdrawals or conversions should not be made until those options are understood.
Pension survivor benefits: If the deceased spouse had a pension, contact the plan administrator immediately. Survivor

elections may be time-sensitive, and the payment structure can have lasting income and tax consequences.

Decisions That Should Usually Wait
The following decisions can usually wait at least six months unless financial necessity makes them urgent.
Selling the house: The home may feel too large, too quiet, or too painful. Those feelings are real. They are not always permanent. A house that feels unbearable at three months may feel essential at twelve.
Major investment changes: Do not rush to simplify the portfolio because the survivor feels overwhelmed. Selling positions may trigger taxes, reduce flexibility, or remove options before the full financial picture is clear.
Large gifts to family: Well-meaning family members may ask for help. The survivor may feel pressure to distribute money quickly. Wait. A survivor who does not yet know the full income, tax, and legal picture should not be making gifts.
New financial relationships: Do not sign with a new advisor, buy new insurance, or commit to new products during acute grief. If the existing relationship is inadequate, that can be addressed later when decisions can be made clearly.

The Tax Changes Nobody Explains

Medicare and IRMAA: The Tax After Death: Medicare premiums can rise when income rises, often with a lag.

A large IRA withdrawal, Roth conversion, required distribution, or one-time income event can push the surviving spouse into higher Medicare premium tiers later.

> **Early Decision Rule**:
> Treat major income moves as a two-year decision.

Before any large IRA withdrawal, Roth conversion, or asset sale, coordinate with the CPA and advisor to understand not only income-tax effects, but Medicare-premium consequences.

Filing Status Changes: After the year of death, filing status usually changes and tax brackets compress. The following year is typically Single filing status, unless the survivor qualifies for Head of Household.

That means the survivor may face higher effective tax pressure even if household income has fallen.

> **Reality Check:**
> The widow's penalty is structural. After the year of death, brackets narrow while RMDs and fixed income often continue. Plan for the survivor's tax bracket, not the couple's.

Required Minimum Distributions Continue: If the deceased spouse was subject to RMDs, the year-of-death RMD generally still must be satisfied if it was not taken before death. After that, the rules depend on how the account is handled and whether the surviving spouse rolls it into their own IRA or keeps it as an inherited account.

The combination of narrower brackets, continued RMDs, and reduced household income is the structural reality.

The Advisor Relationship: What Changes

If the deceased spouse handled the primary relationship with the financial advisor, the dynamic changes immediately. That transition is uncomfortable, but it is also essential.

What the survivor should expect in the first 30 days

- a meeting focused on immediate needs, not investment strategy
- a clear explanation of what assets exist, where they are, and how they transfer
- coordination with the CPA on tax implications, including the final return and the survivor's future filing status

- a written list of time-sensitive decisions and deadlines
- no pressure to make changes that can wait

What the survivor should ask

- What decisions must I make in the next 90 days, and what happens if I delay them?
- How do my income, taxes, and insurance change now?
- What did my spouse understand about the plan that I may not know?
- What is my sustainable spending level under the new reality?
- When should we meet again for the longer-term decisions?

If the advisor cannot answer these questions clearly, or pressures the survivor toward decisions that could wait, that is useful information about the relationship.

What the Primary Decision-Maker Can Do Now

If you are reading this as the spouse who currently manages the financial relationship, this section is for you.

Create the Continuity File: Assemble a single document, physical or digital, that starts with the document inventory from the First Thirty Days section of this chapter. Build it now, while you can. Then add what that list does not cover: digital account access, automatic payments and which accounts fund them, and the contact list for CPA, attorney, advisor, and insurance.

Update this file annually. Review it together.

Have the Conversation: The continuity file answers where things are. The conversation answers why they are structured that way. Both need to happen while you are alive.

The goal is to transfer enough understanding that the surviving spouse can engage confidently with the professionals who will help implement the plan.

Include Your Spouse in Advisory Meetings: Both spouses should attend at least one advisory meeting each year. The survivor should not be meeting the planning team for the first time during a crisis.

Continuity Is a Design Choice

The theme of this book, coordination over fragmentation, structure over hope, applies to survivor continuity as forcefully as it applies to investment design or tax planning.

An estate plan that exists only in documents fails if the surviving spouse cannot find them, understand them, or work with the professionals responsible for implementing them. A financial plan that exists only in one spouse's head is fragile.

Continuity is a design choice made before it matters. Grief does not need to be accompanied by confusion.

Ask Your Advisor Today – Survivor Continuity
First call: If my spouse died tomorrow, who is the first call, and does that person know they are the first call?
Ninety-day walk-through: Walk me through the first ninety days from the survivor's perspective: deadlines, cash sources, and what should not be changed yet.
Relationship continuity: Can you meet with both of us annually, so the surviving spouse has a relationship with the team before it becomes essential?

Chapter 15: Choosing an Advisor: Accountability for Your Retirement System

Volatility had to be contained. Taxes had to be coordinated. Income had to be engineered. Risk had to be transferred before it arrived.

But structure does not maintain itself. Someone has to own the retirement system, coordinate the moving parts, and remain accountable for how decisions interact over time.

That person is the advisor.

What Breaks When Advice Is Fragmented

Every case study that shows damage in this book failed the same way: fragmented coordination.

Each planning domain made sense in isolation. Together, they degraded the system they were supposed to support.

That is what fragmented advice does. One professional optimizes taxes. Another manages investments. Another handles insurance. Another drafted the estate documents years ago. No one owns how those decisions interact. Over time, the client becomes the integrator by default, often at the exact moment integration is hardest: a health event, a death, or cognitive decline.

That is not planning. That is delegation without coordination. The structural reason it persists is that most advisors are not rewarded to fix it.

Early Decision Rule:
The advisor you choose is the only professional whose job is the whole picture. Everyone else owns a piece.

The Advisor's Role: Integrator, Not Optimizer

Good advisors do not eliminate uncertainty. They design systems that remain usable when uncertainty is unavoidable. As retirement progresses, the role shifts from implementation to stewardship. RMDs begin, tax brackets change, Medicare premiums respond to income, and survivor decisions become time sensitive. At those stages, episodic or transactional advice becomes actively harmful. The real test is survivability, not performance. Choosing an advisor is a decision about control, not over markets, but over decisions, behavior, and long-term outcomes. Most people underestimate that. The right advisor's influence on your retirement compounds far more than any single investment recommendation.

Independence Is a Structural Requirement

Independence goes beyond avoiding product bias. It means reducing structural bias: advice that pushes isolated decisions instead of a coordinated plan. An advisor rewarded only for one product, transaction, or account type is structurally less likely to manage the full system well. The first meeting is where you find out which kind you are talking to.

Reality Check:
A first meeting should be a diagnostic, not a presentation. If you leave without clarity on gaps, fees, coordination, and review cadence, it was not planning. It was marketing.

What a Good First Meeting Looks Like

You are not there to hear about the firm's history or its investment philosophy. You are there to determine whether this person thinks about your situation the way it deserves to be thought about.

A good first meeting covers five things:

- your full retirement picture, investments plus income sources, taxes, Medicare and health costs, insurance, estate basics, and spending
- what appears sound and what deserves a closer look, including at least one specific risk the advisor identified from your situation
- how the advisor and firm are fully compensated, including advisory fees, fund expenses, insurance commissions, and referral arrangements
- how coordination works, including whether they work proactively with your CPA, attorney, and insurance professionals or only if you force the issue
- what the ongoing relationship looks like, including meeting cadence, triggers for unscheduled reviews, and how changes are documented and implemented

If you leave a first meeting without knowing those five things, either schedule a second meeting or find someone else.

Advisor Integration Scorecard (0–20 points)

Score each item:

- **0** = not addressed
- **1** = partially addressed
- **2** = addressed with a written policy or deliverable

1. Volatility and spending guardrails are written, including what changes at declines of ten, twenty and thirty percent.
2. A five-year tax map exists, including brackets, IRMAA lookback awareness, Roth windows, and the RMD trajectory.

3. An income plan exists, including sources, start dates, survivor changes, and essential versus discretionary spending.
4. Withdrawal sequencing rules are written and conditional, rather than one-size-fits-all.
5. A health-cost and care-risk plan exists, including Medicare, long-term care exposure, and the funding approach.
6. A cash-access plan exists for the first 90 days of incapacity or death.
7. Beneficiary designations and account titling are reviewed and documented.
8. Specialist coordination is explicit, including the CPA, attorney, and insurance professionals, with one person accountable for follow-through.
9. Governance cadence is defined, including review schedule, triggers for unscheduled action, and written updates.
10. The advisor can explain the entire plan in plain language in five minutes.

Interpretation

- **0–7:** components, not a system
- **8–14:** partial integration
- **15–20:** integrated planning with accountability

What This Means for You:
A score below fifteen does not mean your advisor is incompetent. It means the plan is managed in pieces rather than as a system. The gaps the scorecard identifies are the places where fragmentation damages the plan once stress exposes it.

Ask Your Advisor Today – Choosing an Advisor

One-page system: Can you show me my complete plan on one page, including volatility policy, tax map, income ladder, risk transfer, and governance, and tell me what breaks first in a severe downturn?

Irreversible decisions: Which decisions in my plan are time-sensitive or irreversible, and what is the timeline for each?

Next Twelve Months: What are my three biggest structural gaps, and what specific actions will we take in the next twelve months to close them?

Integration Check: Act V: Control and Continuity

1. If I died this year, walk me through the first ninety days for my spouse: what changes, what must be decided, and what can safely wait.
2. Do my will, trusts, beneficiary designations, and account titling all match, and where is that alignment documented?
3. Who owns the job of coordinating investments, taxes, insurance, and estate planning, and how does that governance continue if my spouse is the one calling alone?
4. If I scored my current plan on the Advisor Integration Scorecard today, what would my score be, and which gaps would I address first?

Conclusion: The Fortress Built

This book began on a trading desk. Hope and prayer were not acceptable risk-management strategies. The only honest response to uncertainty was structure.

Retirement planning operates under the same conditions. Four forces can each dismantle a plan that looks sound on paper. Volatility pressures investors into decisions that turn temporary declines into permanent damage. Taxes, left unmanaged, compound across decades, draining wealth through forced income, compressed brackets, and thresholds that were never modeled. Inflation raises the cost of living year after year, and a plan that does not account for it falls behind gradually and often irreversibly. Non-market risks: long-term care, disability, and premature death, arrive without warning, and their costs cannot be managed through asset allocation alone.

No plan can predict which of these forces will arrive first, or in what combination. All of them can be prepared for. That preparation is what this book is about.

What the Case Studies Showed

Siloed advice and uncoordinated decisions caused the damage. Avoidable taxes. Compressed survivor brackets. Badly funded care. Stress-driven investment decisions. Income plans that looked fine until life forced them to perform. No advisor owned the whole system. Every one of those outcomes was structural.

Integrated planning told a different story. Grant and Susan spent 28.6 percent more per year for decades without reducing the amount left to their heirs. Minnie and Jean reduced taxes from age seventy-three onward by 75 percent with an eight-year conversion window that cost 22.6 cents on the dollar. Big Red's coordinated plan delivered 33 percent more after-tax value to her brother from the same assets and the same spending. Isidore built flexible infrastructure from a single annual premium that funded a business expansion, bridged a Roth conversion window, executed a partner buyout, and in the simplest scenario delivered $3.67 million tax-free to his heirs. Prudence stayed invested through a 38 percent decline because the portfolio was designed for who she actually was. Same assets. Same markets. Different architecture.

The coordinated alternatives used no exotic strategies. They used standard tools. The difference was treating them as one system rather than as separate decisions made in isolation.

The Real Cost of Fragmentation

Fragmentation is invisible until it is not. Each silo can look fine on its own. The investment portfolio is managed. Insurance is in place. Retirement accounts are funded. On paper, every box is checked.

The damage appears at the seams.

It appears when taxes, withdrawals, and income timing collide across decisions that were never designed to work together. When the surviving spouse files as single for the first time and the RMD does not adjust for bracket compression. When the brokerage account is depleted to fund care while the IRA continues growing toward a massive tax bill. When Roth conversions are ignored and the IRA is now far larger than the plan can use efficiently. When inflation raises the spending floor by 40 percent and the income system was never recalibrated.

These are the predictable consequences of competent, credentialed, well-intentioned advice delivered in pieces.

What Coordination Actually Means

Coordination is a discipline. Every decision has to be tested against the full plan. Does it strengthen the fortress against all four risks, or weaken it?

It means the Social Security claiming decision is made in the context of IRA balances, projected RMDs, and the survivor's future bracket, not on a break-even spreadsheet alone. It means the long-term care decision is made with full knowledge of which account will fund care, at what effective tax rate, and at what cost to the heir. It means the portfolio's volatility profile is matched to the investor's actual behavioral tolerance, not to an idealized version of who they should be under stress. And it means inflation is treated as a design constraint from the beginning, not as a surprise that arrives in year fifteen.

None of these ideas are complicated on their own. Their power comes from doing them together, across every domain, across every year of a retirement that may last three decades.

The Question Worth Carrying Forward

If there is one question this book is meant to leave with you, it is this:

Does anyone see the whole picture, and is anyone accountable for how the pieces interact?

Not the portfolio alone. Not the tax return alone. Not the insurance coverage alone. Not the estate documents alone.

The whole system, together, held to the same objectives and tested against the same risks.

If the answer is yes, you already have what most retirement plans are missing. If the answer is no, or if you are not sure, that is the conversation worth having before the window closes.

A fortress protects what is inside it. The financial structure this book describes exists to support a retirement worth living. Purpose, health, relationships, and the things that give your days meaning are why planning matters in the first place. The structure exists so the rest of your life has room to be about more than money.

A Conversation Worth Having

The questions at the end of each chapter and the Advisor Integration Scorecard in Chapter 15 probably raised more questions than they answered. The issues in this book are familiar because they exist in most plans. They need to be addressed before the window to coordinate them closes. The earlier the conversation starts, the more opportunities remain available.

Triathlon Partners LLC works with families facing exactly these issues. The conversation does not begin with products. It begins with structure: where the gaps are, which decisions matter most, and which windows are still open.

www.TriathlonPartners.com | www.TheOriginalIRA.com

TRIATHLON PARTNERS LLC IS A REGISTERED INVESTMENT ADVISER IN THE STATE OF CONNECTICUT. THIS PAGE IS FOR INFORMATIONAL PURPOSES ONLY AND DOES NOT CONSTITUTE AN OFFER OF ADVISORY SERVICES

Appendix

APPENDIX DISCLOSURES
This book is for educational purposes only and is not investment, legal, or tax advice. Charts, tables, case studies, projections, and examples are illustrative and may be hypothetical. They do not represent actual client results and are not a guarantee of any future outcome. Market and economic data, when shown, are believed to come from reliable sources, but accuracy is not guaranteed. Indices are unmanaged and cannot be invested in directly. Index performance does not reflect fees, taxes, or transaction costs. Tax discussions reflect general concepts only. Actual outcomes depend on individual facts, current law, and future changes. Insurance, annuity, and structured product discussions are general. Terms, fees, riders, guarantees, and suitability vary by carrier, issuer, and contract. This appendix supports the illustrations used in the book. It is not a recommendation to implement any specific strategy. Readers should consult qualified financial, tax, and legal professionals before implementing any strategy discussed herein.

Appendix A: Advanced Defined-Outcome Structures

This appendix is for readers and advisors who want the mechanical detail behind Act I. If the chapters gave you enough, skip this entirely. Nothing here changes the planning framework. The payoff reference that follows illustrates the building blocks. The sections after it show how those building blocks are combined, repositioned, and governed inside real portfolio structures.

Example 1: 15% buffer + 13% cap
A buffer absorbs the first layer of loss. In this example, the index can decline up to 15% before the investor absorbs any loss. A

10% decline produces roughly a 0% result. A 25% decline produces roughly a 10% loss. On the upside, gains are capped at 13%. If the index rises 20%, the investor earns 13%. The buffer softens common corrections. The cap is the cost.

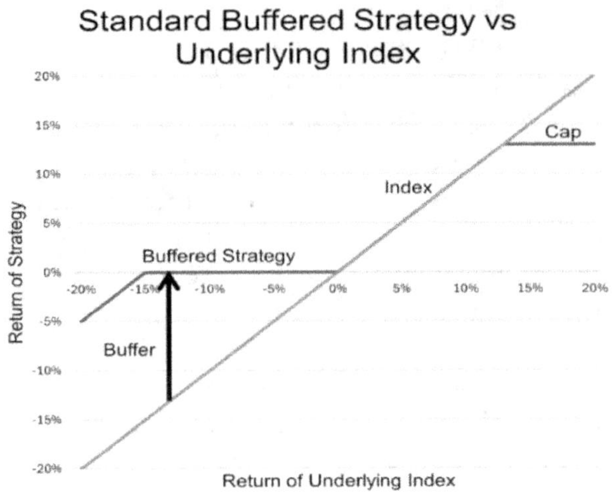

Choose this when the primary objective is surviving common corrections while maintaining upside participation.

Example 2: 10% floor + 11% cap

A floor sets the maximum loss the investor can experience. In this example, the investor absorbs the first 10% of decline. Everything beyond that is absorbed by the structure. Whether the index finishes down 15% or 40%, the loss is limited to approximately 10%. The upside is capped at 11%. The floor provides certainty about the worst case. The investor pays for that certainty by absorbing the initial losses and accepting a lower cap.

Choose this when the priority is a hard ceiling on the worst possible outcome, and the investor can absorb the first layer of loss.

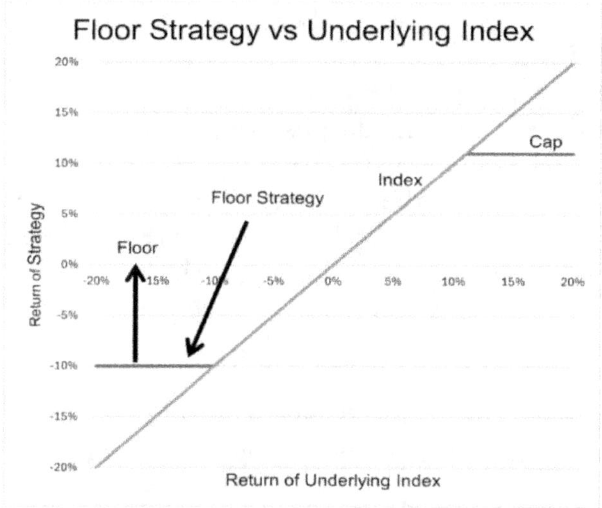

A **participation rate** works differently. Instead of imposing a flat cap, the investor receives a percentage of the index gain. An 80% participation rate on a 10% index gain produces roughly an 8% gain. Participation rates are often used when a hard cap would feel too restrictive or when the payoff design is more complex. The trade-off could be that unlimited upside terms are offset with less protection, more conditionality, or longer maturities.

Engineering the Middle: Step-Up Strategies

Buffers and floors address the depth of loss. A different strategy addresses something more subtle but still corrosive. In markets that are neither crashing nor appreciating, there can be a slow erosion of confidence.

Flat years, mildly negative years, and choppy markets that go nowhere can test an investor's commitment to a retirement plan. The experience of earning or losing a little year after year creates frustration, impatience, and doubt.

A step-up design is built for that environment. If the index finishes positive, even slightly, the structure earns a fixed return. If it finishes down but within the buffer, the result is approximately zero. If it finishes down beyond the buffer, losses resume beyond that threshold.

A step-up turns a wide band of mildly positive and slightly negative outcomes into something more predictable. A small gain, or at least no loss, can be the difference between a frustrating year of staying in place and a year that questions the retirement plan. A variation, the dual step-up, pays a positive return even on mild declines as long as the loss stays within the buffer, widening the range of years that feel productive.

These structures are not the growth engine of a retirement plan. They keep frustrating markets from becoming a reason to abandon the plan.

Example 3: 15% Buffer + 9.5% Step-Up
A step-up pays a fixed return in any year the index finishes positive, regardless of how much it gained. In this example, if the index finishes up 1% or up 25%, the investor earns 9.5% either way. If the index finishes down but within the 15% buffer, the result is approximately zero. If it finishes beyond the buffer, losses are realized beyond that threshold. The step-up replaces variable upside with a predictable positive outcome across a wide range of markets.

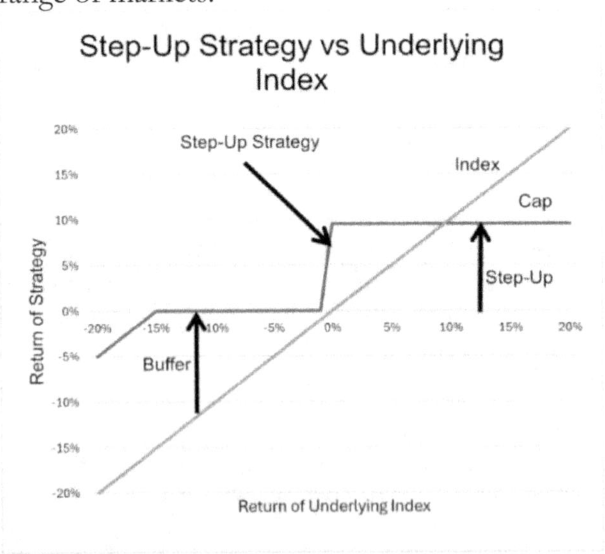

Choose this when the investor wants a predictable positive outcome in any year the market finishes up and can accept giving up strong-rally participation in exchange for that certainty.

Example 4: 15% Buffer + 7.5% Dual Step-Up

A dual step-up pays a fixed return as long as the index finishes above the buffer level at maturity, not just above zero. In this example, the index can decline up to 15% and the investor still earns 7.5%. If the index finishes positive, the same 7.5% is earned regardless of how strong the rally. If the index declines beyond the 15% buffer, losses are realized beyond that threshold. The range of outcomes that produce a positive return is significantly wider than a standard step-up, which only pays when the index finishes above zero.

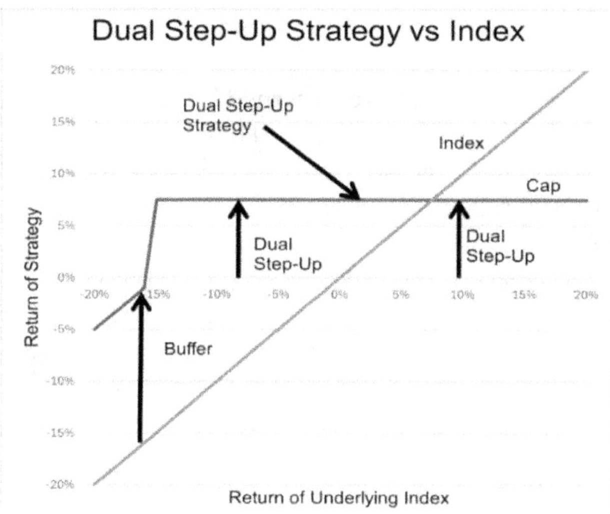

Choose this when you want positive outcomes even through mild declines (roughly to -15%) and are willing to cap strong-rally upside.

Important note: These illustrations are simplified and ignore fees, spreads, taxes, dividends, and issuer-specific terms. Interim values can deviate substantially from the maturity payoff. Protection relies on holding through maturity and on the claims-paying ability of the issuer.

Interim Valuation and Behavior

Defined-outcome strategies are measured from inception to maturity, but they still have daily market values. Protection usually applies to the payoff at maturity, not to interim pricing. Interim values can fall significantly, even in structures that ultimately provide protection at maturity. A buffered or floored strategy may show a large temporary drawdown before recovering into its defined outcome. Investors who focus solely on daily values may still be tempted to abandon a structure at the worst possible time. The behavioral objective is to reduce the magnitude of losses at the measurement points that matter most for the plan, so there are fewer moments that trigger permanent damage.

Governance principles

These strategies work when they are governed by rules established before the investment is made. They fail when maturity decisions are made by emotion, when issuer exposure accumulates without limits, or when structures are added without a portfolio-level rationale.

At each maturity, a governance decision follows. Did the segment fulfill its role? Were the constraints an acceptable tradeoff? Should the proceeds be reinvested in a similar strategy, a different structure, or into open-ended exposure?

Issuer exposure should be capped and diversified across multiple banks or carriers. Maturities should be staggered across years so that the entire defined-outcome allocation does not reset at the same time. Each structure type should have a clear maximum allocation within the portfolio. Actions at maturity or early call should be governed by written rules, not headlines.

Defined-Outcome Vehicles: How the Same Strategy Gets Delivered

The same payoff designs from Act I can be delivered through fundamentally different vehicles. The payoff may look similar on paper. The vehicle determines how that return is affected by taxes, liquidity, and credit exposure.

RILAs / FIAs: Insurance contracts with tax deferral, insurer credit exposure, and often surrender schedules. Tax deferral benefits long-horizon capital, but surrender schedules can penalize early exit.

Indexed Universal Life (IUL): Insurance chassis with a long horizon, policy charges, potential tax-advantaged access, insurer credit exposure, and a death benefit. Structure and costs are covered in Appendix C.

Outcome-defined ETFs: Brokerage wrappers with daily liquidity, transparent pricing, and standardized outcomes. No surrender periods and no insurer credit exposure. Generally lower caps than contract-based alternatives.

Structured notes: Bank-issued contracts with highly customizable outcomes, bank credit exposure, and limited secondary liquidity. The most flexible payoff design, but the least liquid and most credit-dependent.

In practice, long-horizon tax-deferred accounts are natural holders for contract-based layers. Taxable accounts are often better served by liquid, transparent versions of the same ideas. Bank-issued structures with participation multipliers belong in tax-deferred accounts, as their worst-case downside is equivalent to traditional allocations while the multipliers can produce meaningful outperformance.

The sections that follow cover RILA strategies, structured note mechanics, and governance frameworks in detail.

RILA Strategies and Blends

RILAs deliver defined-outcome structures inside a tax-deferred insurance chassis with two features not available elsewhere: intra-term repositioning and multi-strategy blending within the same contract.

Intra-term repositioning: Alexander's RILA reallocation

Alexander purchased a one-year step-up RILA strategy with a 10% buffer and a 10.5% cap. Six months in, the index had risen sharply, and the current value reflected most of the cap already earned. Remaining upside was limited, and the risk-reward profile had changed. Alexander chose to exit early and redeploy into a new strategy with a payoff shape that better fit the remaining horizon. Because this was inside a tax-deferred contract, he could reposition without incurring immediate taxes.

Some contract-based wrappers allow intra-term adjustments without realizing taxable gains. Not all wrappers offer that flexibility, and opportunistic exits require a clear governance process, not impulse.

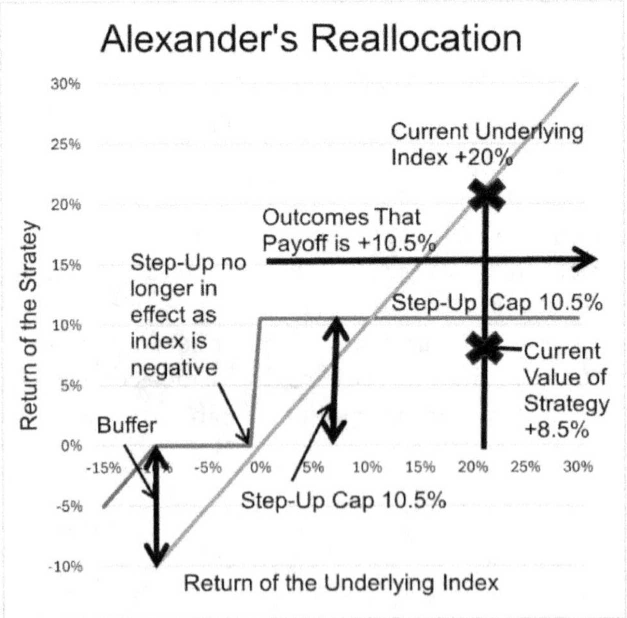

Blending defined-outcome strategies
One advantage of RILA-type structures is the ability to split capital across multiple strategies. For example, an allocation might combine 50% in a dual step-up (15% buffer, 7.5% credit if the index is above -15%), 25% in a standard buffer (20% buffer, 11% cap), and 25% in a step-up (15% buffer, 9.5% credit if the index is positive). Each sleeve operates independently, but together they compress drawdowns across a wider range of negative scenarios, provide small positive outcomes in modest or slightly negative environments, and cap upside in strong rallies.

Blending changes the payoff geometry of that slice of the portfolio. The goal is to narrow the range of outcomes, so the plan remains usable across common market regimes.

Blended payoff outcomes:
When the underlying index is negative, the blended portfolio produces a positive 3.75% return from -15% to 0%, driven by the dual step-up earning its preset return even in moderately negative markets. At -20%, the blended decline is approximately -3.75%, creating an effective buffer of 16.25%. At -30%, the portfolio declines approximately -13.75%, maintaining that 16.25% downside compression relative to the index.

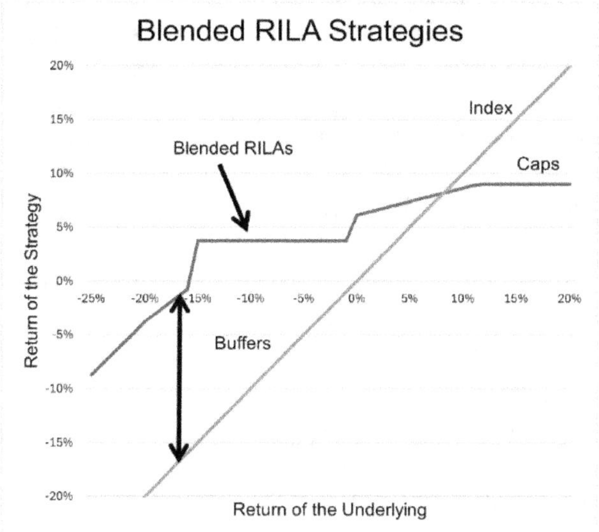

When the underlying index is positive, returns begin at approximately 6.125%, driven by the two step-up allocations. As the index rises, the standard buffer allocation contributes incremental gains, gradually increasing total return to a maximum of approximately 9% when the index is up roughly 12%. Beyond that level, additional upside is capped.

Distribution channels and economics
How a RILA is distributed affects economics. Commission-based versions often embed compensation through lower caps and longer surrender schedules. Fee-based versions may reduce or remove surrender penalties and can offer more favorable terms, but charge asset-based fees instead. Investors experience these differences through caps, participation rates, rider costs, and liquidity, not through a line item labeled "commission".

Structured Notes: Income and Growth

Structured notes are bank-issued obligations with payoffs tied to indexes. They are neither traditional bonds nor direct equity. They are hybrids with distinct risk profiles.

Income notes: cash flow with conditions
Income notes generate contractual cash flow while reshaping downside risk. Coupons are paid only if index-based conditions are met on observation dates. As an illustrative example, a two-year income note linked to the S&P 500 might pay a 9% annual coupon, monthly, if the index is above 70% of its initial level on each observation date. If the index is below the threshold, that month's coupon is skipped but can resume later. At maturity, if the index is at or above 70%, principal is returned. If below, the barrier is breached and losses are realized one-for-one from inception.

Income notes reshape income risk. They do not remove it. They replace interest-rate risk with market-condition risk and issuer credit risk. They often include call features that end the note early when conditions are favorable, creating reinvestment risk. They should be sized and evaluated like hybrid high-yield credit: useful for specific goals, but inappropriate as a core equity substitute.

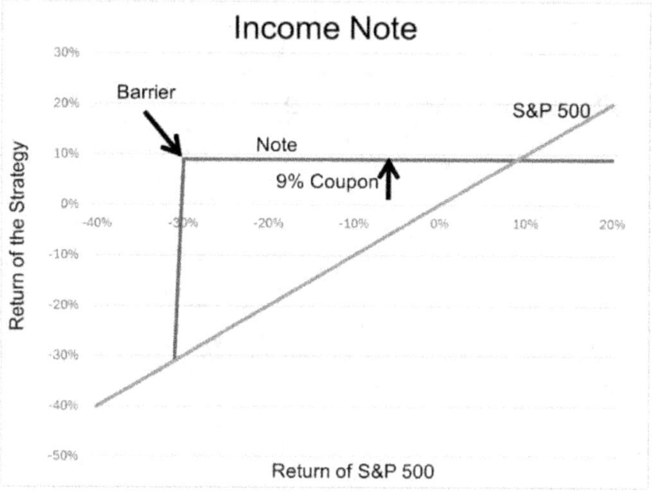

Growth notes: participation with structure

Growth notes target capital appreciation with predefined downside boundaries, usually via barriers, over multi-year holding periods. As an illustrative example, a five-year worst-of growth note linked to the worst performance of two international equity indexes, with a 70% barrier and a 2.25x participation multiplier, works as follows: the lower-performing index determines the result. If that index finishes above 70% of its starting level, full principal is returned and gains are credited at 2.25 times its positive performance. A 30% gain in the worst-performing index becomes roughly a 67.5% return on the note. If it finishes below 70%, protection no longer applies and losses are realized one-for-one from the initial level.

The worst-of design funds the richer upside terms. By accepting the weaker index as the measuring stick, the investor gives the issuer room to offer a higher participation multiplier. The asymmetry cuts both ways. If one index gains 20% but the weaker index finishes down, the stronger performance is irrelevant. The outcome is determined entirely by the weaker index and whether the barrier holds. A weaker index down 20% with a 70% barrier intact returns full principal. A weaker index down 40% breaches the barrier and losses are realized from the initial level. Indexes with broadly similar exposures are usually better suited to this structure.

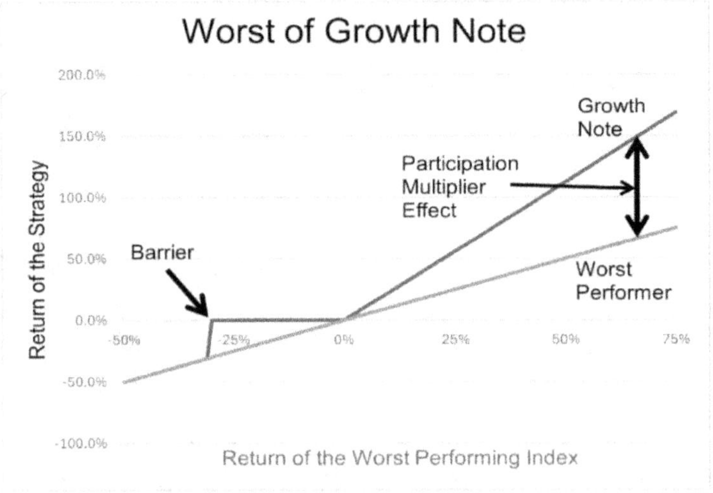

Market re-entry and tactical use

Growth notes may offer structural opportunities after sharp selloffs. Lower index levels translate into lower absolute barrier levels, and higher volatility can improve the terms the issuer offers. These structures are tools for a small, clearly defined opportunity sleeve, not vehicles for the money that must fund essential retirement spending.

Pricing, valuation, and liquidity

Structured note pricing is driven by interest rates, implied volatility, and the cost of hedging the embedded options. Notes have daily market values, but secondary-market prices can differ from the expected maturity payoff. Liquidity is at the issuer's or dealer's discretion, not guaranteed by an exchange. Assume you will hold to maturity when sizing a note. Any early exit should be viewed as a flexibility option, not a design feature you depend on.

Failure modes
Structured notes rarely break down because the math was misunderstood. They break down because the implementation rules were never formalized. The most common problems are issuer concentration across multiple notes, credit risk if the issuing bank defaults, reinvestment clustering when many maturities hit at the same time, the assumption that secondary liquidity will match maturity terms, and accumulating multiple structure types without a portfolio-level rationale.

Tax treatment varies by note design. In a taxable account, stated or imputed interest is generally ordinary income, while gain or loss on sale or redemption is generally capital gain or loss, subject to exceptions. In a tax-deferred account, taxes are generally deferred until distributions. The offering document's tax considerations section should be reviewed with your advisor and CPA before making any assumptions.

Appendix B: Alternative Retirement Vehicles

Health Savings Accounts (HSAs)
An HSA is available to individuals enrolled in a high-deductible health care plan. It is a triple-tax-advantaged account: contributions are tax deductible, growth is tax-free, and withdrawals for qualified medical expenses are tax-free.

HSAs are powerful when treated as long-term retirement assets. If a household can pay current medical expenses out of pocket, the HSA can remain invested and compound tax-free for years.

HSAs are not subject to required minimum distributions.

529 Plans (Education)
A 529 plan works like a Roth for education. Contributions are not federally deductible, but growth is tax-free and withdrawals are tax-free for qualified education expenses. In a taxable account, education savings would generate ongoing tax drag

from dividends and interest, and capital gains at withdrawal. A 529 removes both. Like HSAs, 529 plans are not subject to required minimum distributions.

Properly Structured Cash-Value Life Insurance
When designed and funded properly, certain cash-value policies can provide tax-deferred growth and tax-advantaged access to accumulated cash value. Unlike qualified retirement accounts, premiums are not subject to IRS contribution ceilings. There are also no required minimum distributions. Since the structure is an insurance contract, it includes a death benefit as well.

This is a strategy with distinct trade-offs, covered in the insurance chapter.

Long-Term Care Planning
Long-term care insurance benefits are typically received tax-free. Without dedicated coverage, care expenses often force taxable asset sales or tax-deferred withdrawals, increasing bracket pressure.

Appendix C: Insurance Policy Design and Mechanics

Policy Design: Death Benefit and MEC Thresholds
A permanent insurance contract balances death benefit with an investment component. For a given premium, the death benefit can vary depending on the needs of the insured. Where it is set determines what the contract can do over a lifetime.

The maximum death benefit is set by the insurer. More of every premium dollar pays for insurance charges and less is available to invest. Cash value grows slowly. Protection starts large. Flexibility starts small.

The minimum death benefit is set by the IRS. Since insurance contracts grow tax-deferred and policy loans allow for tax-exempt access, the IRS regulates the ratio of premium to death benefit. If too much premium is paid relative to the death benefit, the policy becomes a Modified Endowment Contract, or MEC. MEC status makes loans and withdrawals taxable. Staying below the MEC threshold preserves the policy's most valuable feature: tax-advantaged access to cash value. For a 40-year-old, the maximum death benefit can be roughly three times the non-MEC minimum.

Structuring a permanent contract to minimize insurance costs and invest the maximum IRS-allowable amount builds cash value efficiently. That cash value, accessible through tax-exempt loans, creates the infrastructure the chapter describes.

Accessing Cash Value: Withdrawals and Loans
Cash value can be accessed through a combination of withdrawals and policy loans. Withdrawals up to basis are generally not taxed. Loans are not treated as taxable income as long as the policy remains in force and is not a Modified Endowment Contract. The tax advantage is not automatic. It depends on policy structure, MEC status, and loan management over the life of the contract.

Appendix D: Model Assumptions and Tables

The examples in this book are simplified illustrations used to show how structure changes outcomes. They use round numbers and simplified assumptions so that the planning logic stays visible. Real plans require updated tax rules, actual account values, current product terms, family facts, and legal review. The case studies are best read as structural comparisons, not point estimates. The important questions are which account is being used, when the tax is being paid, who bears the tax later, what flexibility remains, and whether the surviving spouse or heir is left with a system that still functions.

Common assumptions across all case studies: 2026 federal income tax brackets per IRS Revenue Procedure 2025-32 as adjusted by the One Big Beautiful Bill Act. Standard deduction of $32,200 married filing jointly, $16,100 single. Additional standard deduction of $1,650 per person age 65 and older. Senior deduction of $6,000 per qualifying person age 65 and older, phasing out at 6% of adjusted gross income above $150,000 married filing jointly or $75,000 single.

Required minimum distributions per the Uniform Lifetime Table, beginning at age 73. All growth rates, brackets, and thresholds are held constant. No inflation adjustment to spending, Social Security, or tax parameters. No sequence-of-return risk. No advisory fees. No estate tax unless stated. Each model isolates the structural decisions from all other variables.

D1. Grant and Susan – Model Assumptions

Starting balances at age 62: Traditional IRA $3,500,000. Brokerage $1,000,000 with cost basis of $700,000 (unrealized gain $300,000). Roth $0.
Growth rates: IRA and Roth 7.0% annually. Brokerage 6.0% annually, net of tax drag on dividends and rebalancing.
Spending: $150,000 per year after federal tax and IRMAA surcharges. Spending need increases by the IRMAA amount in years when surcharges apply, so lifestyle spending remains constant at $150,000.
Social Security: Grant full retirement age benefit $42,000 annually. Susan full retirement age benefit $18,000 annually. DIY scenario: both claim at 62 with standard 30% permanent reduction ($29,400 and $12,600). Advisor scenario: Grant delays to 70 ($52,080), Susan claims at 62 ($12,600). Survivor benefit equals the deceased spouse's claimed benefit amount.
No state income tax (Florida).
Capital gains: Long-term capital gains taxed at 15% plus 3.8% net investment income tax, for a combined rate of 18.8%. Brokerage withdrawals use proportional basis tracking. Each withdrawal realizes gain equal to the withdrawal amount multiplied by the account's current gain ratio. Basis does not grow with market appreciation.
Medicare IRMAA: 2026 thresholds per CMS. Surcharges based on modified adjusted gross income from two years prior. Parts B and D combined. Both spouses assessed during the couple phase. One survivor assessed during the survivor phase.
Conversion strategy (advisor scenario): Phase 1, age 62 conversions fill to top of 24% bracket ($403,550 taxable income). Phase 2, ages 63 through 79, conversions target MAGI at or below $342,000. No conversions at age 80.
Spending source (advisor scenario): Living expenses funded from brokerage account first, generating long-term capital gains on the gain portion only. When brokerage is depleted, spending is funded from Roth. Conversion tax paid from brokerage when available, otherwise from Roth. All IRA outflow during the conversion phase goes to Roth.
Spending source (DIY scenario): Living expenses funded from IRA withdrawals plus Social Security. RMD surplus deposited to brokerage at full cost basis.
Survivor assumptions: One spouse dies at 80. Surviving spouse files as single from age 81. Spousal rollover of decedent's IRA. Brokerage receives step-up in basis on decedent's half. Roth continues. Survivor receives the higher of the two Social Security benefits.
Heir value: IRA valued at 50% to reflect the heir's combined federal, and state marginal tax rate under the 10-year distribution rule. Brokerage receives step-up in basis at death. Roth passes tax-free.

D2. Big Red – Optimized and No-Action Tables

Single female, age 62 at retirement. Pension: $50,000 annually. Traditional IRA: $1,750,000. Social Security: $30,000 if claimed at 62, $53,143 if delayed to 70. Brokerage: $0 at retirement. Brother Dash is sole beneficiary.
Growth rate: IRA and Roth 7.0% annually.

Spending: $80,000 per year after federal tax through age 86. At age 87, long-term care costs increase total spending to approximately $230,000 per year (care plus living expenses) through age 90.
No-action scenario: Social Security claimed at 62 ($30,000). IRA untouched until RMDs begin at 73. Living expenses funded from pension and Social Security. RMD surplus deposited to taxable brokerage at full cost basis. Care costs at ages 87 through 90 funded from brokerage. No long-term care insurance. No Roth conversions.
Coordinated scenario: Social Security delayed to 70 ($53,143). Roth conversions ages 62 through 83, filling to the top of the 24% bracket ($216,775 AGI). Conversion tax paid from converted amount. Living expenses funded from pension, Social Security (beginning at 70), and Roth withdrawals as needed. Long-term care policy purchased at age 62: $12,710 annual premium for 10 years ($127,100 total), producing approximately $600,000 in tax-free benefits during the care event at ages 87 through 90. Insurance benefits fund care costs. Roth funds remaining spending shortfalls.
No state income tax assumed.
Heir value: IRA taxed at 45% to reflect Dash's combined federal and state marginal tax rate under the 10-year distribution rule. Brokerage receives step-up in basis at death. Roth passes tax-free.
IRMAA: Referenced in prose but not included in the analysis.

D3. Minnie and Jean – Model Assumptions

Starting profile at age 62: Pension $80,000 annually. Social Security $40,000 per spouse ($80,000 combined). Traditional IRA $1,885,976, the balance that grows at 7% annually to produce a $140,000 RMD at age 73.
Growth rate: IRA and Roth 7.0% annually. Brokerage 7.0% annually.
Spending: $128,582 per year after federal tax. Held constant throughout.
Social Security claiming: One spouse claims at 62 ($40,000). The other delays to age 70 ($71,000). Survivor benefit equals the delayed benefit of $71,000.
Conversion strategy: Ages 62 through 69, convert to the top of the 24% married-filing-jointly bracket. Blended conversion rate 22.6%. Total conversion tax paid $570,477. Traditional IRA reaches $0 at end of age 69.
Balances at age 72: Traditional IRA $0. Roth $2,453,543. Brokerage $33,123 (funded by post-tax surplus income beginning at age 70).
Surplus income: Beginning at age 70, combined after-tax income exceeds lifestyle need by $10,303 per year. Surplus deposited to taxable brokerage.
Survivor assumptions: One spouse dies at age 73. Surviving spouse files as single. Pension continues. Survivor receives the $71,000 delayed Social Security benefit. No RMDs in the planned scenario. Unplanned scenario assumes both spouses claimed at 62 ($40,000 survivor benefit) with full $140,000 RMD beginning at 73.
No state income tax assumed.
IRMAA: Referenced in chapter prose but not included in the tables. Planned survivor at $151,000 income pays $2,874 annually. Unplanned survivor at $260,000 income pays $6,292 annually.
Heir value: IRA taxed at 37%. Brokerage receives step-up in basis at death. Roth passes tax-free.

D4. Isidore -- Model Assumptions

Male, age 40 at policy inception. Premium: $15,000 per year for 30 years in all scenarios.
Max Death Benefit contract: initial death benefit $1,904,556. Max Non-MEC contract: initial death benefit $675,647. Blended structure: $1,475 per year to 20-year term

($1,300,000 death benefit), $13,525 per year to Max Non-MEC permanent contract ($610,000 initial death benefit). At term expiration (age 60), redirected premium increases permanent contract funding to $25,280 per year for five years.
Illustrated index return: 6.47% average annual return before policy charges in all scenarios. Actual performance will depend on caps, participation rates, fees, and policy design.
Policy loans are absorbed by the policy's cash value growth and secured by the death benefit. Scenario 1 (business expansion): $1,000,000 policy loan. Scenario 2 (Roth conversion bridge): $120,000 per year in policy loans for seven years, $840,000 total. Scenario 3 (partner buyout): $1,650,000 single policy loan. Scenario 4 (leave it alone): no loans, no withdrawals. Death benefit at age 90: $3,671,157.
Cash value and death benefit figures are hypothetical illustrations based on the assumed return rate and policy structure described. They are not guarantees. Actual results depend on carrier, contract terms, market conditions, and policy management. Tax treatment of policy loans assumes the contract is not a Modified Endowment Contract and remains in force. See Appendix Disclosures.

Big Red Optimized Scenario

Age	Pension	SS	Tax SS	RMD	IRA Dist	AGI	Tax	M %	After-Tax
62	$50,000	$0	$0	$0	$166,775	$216,775	$51,863	24	$164,912
63	$50,000	$0	$0	$0	$166,775	$216,775	$51,863	24	$164,912
64	$50,000	$0	$0	$0	$166,775	$216,775	$51,863	24	$164,912
65	$50,000	$0	$0	$0	$166,775	$216,775	$51,863	24	$164,912
66	$50,000	$0	$0	$0	$166,775	$216,775	$51,863	24	$164,912
67	$50,000	$0	$0	$0	$166,775	$216,775	$51,863	24	$164,912
68	$50,000	$0	$0	$0	$166,775	$216,775	$51,863	24	$164,912
69	$50,000	$0	$0	$0	$166,775	$216,775	$51,863	24	$164,912
70	$50,000	$53,143	$45,172	$0	$121,603	$216,775	$51,863	24	$172,883
71	$50,000	$53,143	$45,172	$0	$121,603	$216,775	$51,863	24	$172,883
72	$50,000	$53,143	$45,172	$0	$121,603	$216,775	$51,863	24	$172,883
73	$50,000	$53,143	$45,172	$38,578	$121,603	$216,775	$51,863	24	$172,883
74	$50,000	$53,143	$45,172	$37,794	$121,603	$216,775	$51,863	24	$172,883
75	$50,000	$53,143	$45,172	$36,630	$121,603	$216,775	$51,863	24	$172,883
76	$50,000	$53,143	$45,172	$35,192	$121,603	$216,775	$51,863	24	$172,883
77	$50,000	$53,143	$45,172	$33,290	$121,603	$216,775	$51,863	24	$172,883
78	$50,000	$53,143	$45,172	$31,163	$121,603	$216,775	$51,863	24	$172,883
79	$50,000	$53,143	$45,172	$28,600	$121,603	$216,775	$51,863	24	$172,883
80	$50,000	$53,143	$45,172	$25,524	$121,603	$216,775	$51,863	24	$172,883
81	$50,000	$53,143	$45,172	$21,730	$121,603	$216,775	$51,863	24	$172,883
82	$50,000	$53,143	$45,172	$17,348	$121,603	$216,775	$51,863	24	$172,883
83	$50,000	$53,143	$45,172	$12,051	$121,603	$216,775	$51,863	24	$172,883
84	$50,000	$53,143	$45,172	$5,840	$98,111	$193,283	$45,085	24	$156,169
85	$50,000	$53,143	$45,172	$0	$0	$95,172	$17,108	22	$86,035
86	$50,000	$53,143	$45,172	$0	$0	$95,172	$17,108	22	$86,035
87	$50,000	$53,143	$45,172	$0	$0	$95,172	$17,108	22	$86,035
88	$50,000	$53,143	$45,172	$0	$0	$95,172	$17,108	22	$86,035
89	$50,000	$53,143	$45,172	$0	$0	$95,172	$17,108	22	$86,035
90	$50,000	$53,143	$45,172	$0	$0	$95,172	$17,108	22	$86,035
TOTAL	**$1,450,000**	**$1,116,003**	**$948,603**	**$263,443**	**$3,134,759**	**$5,533,362**	**$1,288,722**		**$4,412,040**

Big Red Optimized Scenario

Age	Spending	LTC Prem	Roth←Pull	Roth→Add	IRA Bal	Roth Bal	Heir Value
62	$68,203	$12,710	$0	$83,999	$1,694,051	$89,879	$1,021,607
63	$68,203	$12,710	$0	$83,999	$1,634,185	$186,049	$1,084,851
64	$68,203	$12,710	$0	$83,999	$1,570,129	$288,952	$1,152,523
65	$68,203	$12,710	$0	$83,999	$1,501,589	$399,057	$1,224,931
66	$68,203	$12,710	$0	$83,999	$1,428,250	$516,870	$1,302,408
67	$68,203	$12,710	$0	$83,999	$1,349,779	$642,930	$1,385,308
68	$68,203	$12,710	$0	$83,999	$1,265,814	$777,814	$1,474,012
69	$68,203	$12,710	$0	$83,999	$1,175,972	$922,140	$1,568,925
70	$68,203	$12,710	$0	$91,970	$1,128,174	$1,085,098	$1,705,594
71	$68,203	$12,710	$0	$91,970	$1,077,031	$1,259,464	$1,851,830
72	$68,203	$0	$0	$104,680	$1,022,307	$1,459,634	$2,021,903
73	$142,627	$0	$0	$30,256	$963,753	$1,594,183	$2,124,247
74	$147,781	$0	$0	$25,102	$901,100	$1,732,635	$2,228,240
75	$152,775	$0	$0	$20,108	$834,061	$1,875,436	$2,334,169
76	$158,075	$0	$0	$14,808	$762,330	$2,022,561	$2,441,843
77	$163,276	$0	$0	$9,607	$685,577	$2,174,421	$2,551,488
78	$169,212	$0	$0	$3,671	$603,452	$2,330,558	$2,662,457
79	$175,181	$0	$2,298	$0	$515,578	$2,491,239	$2,774,807
80	$181,479	$0	$8,596	$0	$421,552	$2,656,429	$2,888,283
81	$187,541	$0	$14,658	$0	$320,945	$2,826,695	$3,003,215
82	$194,559	$0	$21,676	$0	$213,296	$3,001,371	$3,118,684
83	$201,229	$0	$28,346	$0	$98,111	$3,181,137	$3,235,098
84	$209,020	$0	$52,851	$0	$0	$3,347,266	$3,347,266
85	$216,311	$0	$130,276	$0	$0	$3,442,179	$3,442,179
86	$223,891	$0	$137,856	$0	$0	$3,535,625	$3,535,625
87	$381,751	$0	$145,716	$0	$0	$3,627,202	$3,627,202
88	$389,973	$0	$153,938	$0	$0	$3,716,392	$3,716,392
89	$399,757	$0	$163,722	$0	$0	$3,801,356	$3,801,356
90	$408,292	$0	$172,257	$0	$0	$3,883,135	$3,883,135
TOTAL	**$4,852,963**	**$127,100**	**$1,239,719**	**$1,050,344**	**$0**	**$3,883,135**	**$3,883,135**

Big Red No-Action Scenario

Age	Pension	SS	Tax SS	RMD Req	AGI	Taxes	M%	After-Tax
62	$50,000	$30,000	$25,500	$0	$75,500	$11,797	22	$68,203
63	$50,000	$30,000	$25,500	$0	$75,500	$11,797	22	$68,203
64	$50,000	$30,000	$25,500	$0	$75,500	$11,797	22	$68,203
65	$50,000	$30,000	$25,500	$0	$75,500	$11,797	22	$68,203
66	$50,000	$30,000	$25,500	$0	$75,500	$11,797	22	$68,203
67	$50,000	$30,000	$25,500	$0	$75,500	$11,797	22	$68,203
68	$50,000	$30,000	$25,500	$0	$75,500	$11,797	22	$68,203
69	$50,000	$30,000	$25,500	$0	$75,500	$11,797	22	$68,203
70	$50,000	$30,000	$25,500	$0	$75,500	$11,797	22	$68,203
71	$50,000	$30,000	$25,500	$0	$75,500	$11,797	22	$68,203
72	$50,000	$30,000	$25,500	$0	$75,500	$11,797	22	$68,203
73	$50,000	$30,000	$25,500	$139,000	$214,500	$51,203	24	$167,797
74	$50,000	$30,000	$25,500	$148,730	$224,903	$54,870	32	$173,860
75	$50,000	$30,000	$25,500	$158,494	$235,412	$58,758	32	$179,735
76	$50,000	$30,000	$25,500	$168,873	$246,611	$62,902	32	$185,971
77	$50,000	$30,000	$25,500	$179,116	$257,757	$67,026	32	$192,090
78	$50,000	$30,000	$25,500	$190,783	$270,415	$71,709	32	$199,073
79	$50,000	$30,000	$25,500	$203,170	$283,890	$77,075	35	$206,095
80	$50,000	$30,000	$25,500	$216,316	$298,228	$82,811	35	$213,505
81	$50,000	$30,000	$25,500	$229,072	$312,290	$88,435	35	$220,637
82	$50,000	$30,000	$25,500	$243,782	$328,425	$94,889	35	$228,892
83	$50,000	$30,000	$25,500	$257,899	$344,101	$101,160	35	$236,739
84	$50,000	$30,000	$25,500	$274,309	$362,211	$108,403	35	$245,906
85	$50,000	$30,000	$25,500	$289,842	$379,598	$115,358	35	$254,484
86	$50,000	$30,000	$25,500	$306,051	$397,825	$122,649	35	$263,401
87	$50,000	$30,000	$25,500	$322,926	$416,897	$130,278	35	$272,648
88	$50,000	$30,000	$25,500	$337,964	$430,310	$135,643	35	$282,321
89	$50,000	$30,000	$25,500	$356,015	$446,660	$142,183	35	$293,832
90	$50,000	$30,000	$25,500	$371,569	$460,441	$147,696	35	$303,874
TOTAL	**$1,450,000**	**$870,000**	**$739,500**	**$4,393,909**	**$6,740,973**	**$1,842,817**		**$4,871,092**

Big Red No-Action Scenario

Age	Spending	Brokerage	Basis	Gains	IRA Bal	Total Pre-Tax	Heir Value
62	$68,203	$0	$0	$0	$1,872,500	$1,872,500	$1,029,875
63	$68,203	$0	$0	$0	$2,003,575	$2,003,575	$1,101,966
64	$68,203	$0	$0	$0	$2,143,825	$2,143,825	$1,179,104
65	$68,203	$0	$0	$0	$2,293,893	$2,293,893	$1,261,641
66	$68,203	$0	$0	$0	$2,454,466	$2,454,466	$1,349,956
67	$68,203	$0	$0	$0	$2,626,278	$2,626,278	$1,444,453
68	$68,203	$0	$0	$0	$2,810,118	$2,810,118	$1,545,565
69	$68,203	$0	$0	$0	$3,006,826	$3,006,826	$1,653,754
70	$68,203	$0	$0	$0	$3,217,304	$3,217,304	$1,769,517
71	$68,203	$0	$0	$0	$3,442,515	$3,442,515	$1,893,383
72	$68,203	$0	$0	$0	$3,683,491	$3,683,491	$2,025,920
73	$142,627	$26,931	$25,170	$1,762	$3,792,606	$3,819,537	$2,112,864
74	$147,781	$56,721	$51,248	$5,473	$3,898,947	$3,955,668	$2,201,142
75	$152,775	$89,539	$78,209	$11,330	$4,002,285	$4,091,824	$2,290,796
76	$158,075	$125,655	$106,104	$19,551	$4,101,751	$4,227,406	$2,381,618
77	$163,276	$165,281	$134,918	$30,364	$4,197,220	$4,362,501	$2,473,752
78	$169,212	$208,802	$164,779	$44,023	$4,286,888	$4,495,690	$2,566,591
79	$175,181	$256,497	$195,693	$60,804	$4,369,578	$4,626,075	$2,659,765
80	$181,479	$308,719	$227,719	$81,000	$4,443,991	$4,752,710	$2,752,914
81	$187,541	$365,741	$260,814	$104,927	$4,509,963	$4,875,705	$2,846,221
82	$194,559	$428,081	$295,148	$132,932	$4,564,814	$4,992,895	$2,938,728
83	$201,229	$496,043	$330,659	$165,384	$4,608,399	$5,104,442	$3,030,663
84	$209,020	$570,234	$367,545	$202,689	$4,637,476	$5,207,710	$3,120,846
85	$216,311	$650,995	$405,718	$245,277	$4,651,968	$5,302,963	$3,209,577
86	$223,891	$738,840	$445,228	$293,613	$4,650,132	$5,388,972	$3,296,413
87	$381,751	$673,819	$379,482	$294,337	$4,630,111	$5,303,930	$3,220,380
88	$389,973	$605,799	$318,855	$286,945	$4,592,596	$5,198,396	$3,131,727
89	$399,757	$534,865	$263,102	$271,763	$4,533,142	$5,068,007	$3,028,093
90	$408,292	$460,577	$211,738	$248,839	$4,452,883	$4,913,460	$2,909,663
TOTAL	**$4,852,963**	**$460,577**	**$211,738**	**$248,839**	**$4,452,883**	**$4,913,460**	**$2,909,663**

About the Author

Ira Koyner has experienced many of the financial-planning challenges this book addresses. He has funded college educations for his children, cared for aging parents, planned for his own retirement, and worked to provide long-term financial security for a child with special needs. Those experiences helped shape both this book and the way he works with clients.

Professionally, Ira spent nearly three decades as a currency options trader at large global banks. That background in institutional risk management runs through this book.

Ira is the founder of Triathlon Partners LLC, a Connecticut-based registered investment adviser and independent insurance brokerage. The firm's integrated approach of coordinating investments, taxes, income, insurance, and estate reflects the planning philosophy described in these pages. He holds a degree from the Wharton School of Business at the University of Pennsylvania.

If the questions this book raises feel relevant to your own plan, he welcomes the conversation at www.FinancialFortress.net.

www.TriathlonPartners.com | www.TheOriginalIRA.com

The Financial Fortress Series

The principles in this book apply across every stage of the planning lifecycle. The coordination problems that shape retirement planning also appear earlier in the wealth-building years, inside closely held businesses, and in estates with greater complexity, concentration, and tax exposure.

Future books in this series will extend the same framework to three additional groups:

High-net-worth individuals and families
Where estate structure, trusts, concentrated assets, tax exposure, philanthropy, beneficiary design, and transfer strategy require a deeper level of coordination. The focus will be on preserving control, liquidity, and clarity when wealth is substantial and the cost of fragmentation is higher.

Business owners
Where income, enterprise value, succession, liquidity, key-person risk, and exit planning are often the same problem viewed from different angles. The focus will be on continuity: how to protect the business, the owner, and the retirement plan when operations, ownership, and family goals all interact.

Planners in the wealth-building years
Where the most valuable planning windows are often open the longest and noticed the least. The focus will be on building the right foundation early: savings structure, tax positioning, insurance design, ownership decisions, and the systems that make later retirement, protection, and legacy planning far more efficient.

The planning problems change. The need for coordination does not.

www.ingramcontent.com/pod-product-compliance
Lightning Source LLC
LaVergne TN
LVHW022217200926
848481LV00006B/1998